HONEST QUESTIONS

HONEST QUESTIONS

pastoral answers to everyday questions

EDITED BY MARK HALLOCK

 ACOMA PRESS

Honest Questions: Pastoral Answers to Everyday Questions

Copyright © 2020 by The Calvary Family of Churches

Published 2020 by Acoma Press

All rights reserved. No part of this publication may be reduced, stored in a retrieval system, or transmitted in any form by any means, electronic, mechanical, photocopy, recording, or otherwise, without the prior permission of the publisher, except as provided for by USA copyright law.

Unless otherwise noted, all Bible references are from the ESV® Bible (The Holy Bible, English Standard Version®), copyright © 2001 by Crossway, a publishing ministry of Good News Publishers. Used by permission. All rights reserved.

Requests for information should be addressed to:

Acoma Press
40 W. Littleton Blvd. Suite 210, PMB 215
Littleton, CO 80120

www.acomapress.org
info@acomapress.org

Cover Design & Interior Layout: Evan Skelton

First Printing, 2020

Printed in the United States of America

Paperback ISBN: 978-1-7341644-6-6
PDF ISBN: 978-1-7341644-7-3

CONTENTS

Contents   5

Introduction   7

PART ONE
HONEST QUESTIONS ABOUT GOD'S WORD   11

1. Can I really trust the Bible?
   (Matt Whitacre)   13

2. Why is the Bible so violent but Jesus so loving?
   (Adam Embry)   23

3. Is Jesus really the only way to be saved?
   (Garrett Wishall)   31

4. How can I comprehend that God is three-in-one?
   (Franck Corbiere)   39

PART TWO
HONEST QUESTIONS ABOUT GOD'S CHURCH   45

5. Can I love Jesus but not the Church?
   (Michael Morgan)   47

6. How do I find a good church?
   (Mark Hallock)   57

7. Why do we celebrate the Lord's Supper every week?
   (Nathan Piotrowski)   65

8. How do I engage practically in the mission of God?
   (Seth Van Essen)   75

9. What is my role in global missions?
   (Kevin Hasenack)   85

10. What does the Bible have to say about social justice?
   (Spencer Parish) — 91

PART THREE
HONEST QUESTIONS ABOUT THE GOD-CENTERED LIFE 99

11. If I gave my life to Jesus, why is my life so hard?
    (Dan Freng) — 101

12. Why does God care about my sex life?
    (Evan Skelton) — 111

13. How can I be more Christ-like in my communication?
    (Jordan Branch) — 123

14. How can I improve my prayer life?
    (Dave Herre) — 131

15. What does it mean to be a joyful Christian?
    (Mat Leonard) — 139

16. If I am saved by grace, why does it matter how I live?
    (Gabe Reed) — 149

Contributors — 155
Notes — 157

INTRODUCTION

Questions.

We all have them.

In particular, many of us have questions about God. Lots of them.

But where do we go to find reliable answers to these questions? Where do we find voices that will speak truth into our doubts and fears? Where can we hear helpful, credible, thoughtful, trustworthy teachers who are concerned not with adding to the confusion, but shining light into it?

Let's be honest. It's not hard in our day to find people tweeting or blogging their opinions about a host of different issues and questions regarding who God is, what He is like, and how He works in the world. But if you are like me, I'm not simply interested in hearing anyone and everyone's opinions on these things. I desire the truth. I don't want to live my life buying into the thoughts and opinions of our ever-changing culture. I desire to align my life and convictions with the truth of our ever-lasting, never-changing God.

That is why this book was written.

To help you find truth in the midst of your questions.

In the following pages, you will hear from 16 different pastors, each answering a common question about God and our relationship to Him. Let me assure you, every pastor who has contributed to this book is an individual who loves God, loves people, and loves His truth. Each of these men are experienced pastors who love ministering to folks, like each of us, who wrestle with honest questions.

In these pages you will not find condemnation, but grace, love, honesty, and clarity.

In these pages you will find truth.

How to Get the Most Out of This Book

Before we get started, let me offer three suggestions to help you get the most out of this book:

#1. Take your time.

At the end of each chapter, we have provided a few questions for personal reflection and discussion. To get the most out of this book, you may want to set aside intentional, unrushed time to pray through and meditate on these. This time of thoughtful and prayerful reflection will be important as you seek to digest and then integrate the material of each chapter into your life and relationship with God.

#2. Read it all the way through or one chapter at a time.

You may want to start at the very beginning of this book and work your way through it chapter by chapter to the end. On the other hand, you may be wrestling with a specific question addressed in this book and want to read that particular chapter first. I would encourage you to use this book however you wish. Each chapter stands on its own, so feel free to jump around as you desire.

#3. Buy a journal...and use it!

I highly recommend picking up a journal of some sort to record your thoughts, prayers, and meditations as you work through this book. It will be helpful to have all of your thoughts in one place as you journal and interact with the questions. Your journal will also be useful as you interact with others about what you are reading and learning.

#4. Think about inviting someone to join you.

While you may choose to work through this book on your own, you may also want to consider asking someone to read it with you. There can be great value in asking your spouse, a pastor, a mentor, or a friend to join you in your study. So often God uses other people to help us grow. Other people in your life can bring helpful insight and perspective you could never get on your own.

Above all, my prayer is that God will use this book to encourage you, comfort you, and enlighten you in the truth. He can handle your questions. All of them. More than that, in the midst of your questions, He loves to help you discover and rejoice in His truth. May He use these pages as a tool to that end.

For God's glory and your joy in Him,

MARK HALLOCK
Lead Pastor, Calvary Church - Englewood, Englewood, CO
President, Calvary Family of Churches

part one

HONEST QUESTIONS ABOUT...

GOD'S WORD

Chapter 1

CAN I REALLY TRUST THE BIBLE?

Matt Whitacre

> The grass withers, the flower fades, but the word of our God will stand forever. (Isaiah 40:8)

It is no secret the Bible has influenced governments, societies and individuals for thousands of years. Containing beautiful works of poetry and a radical but compelling story of redemption, the 66 books of the Bible have inspired and infuriated generations of people. Christians are especially obsessed with it, with some spending their whole lives studying its words. With so much invested, how can Christians know that it is true and reliable? And what relevance does a series of texts, thousands of years old, have on the modern person's life? These are the questions we will explore in this short chapter, observing that the Bible is the historically reliable, written Word of God for the whole world.

The Bible is historically reliable.

The story of the Bible is an incredible journey. Beginning in about 1400 BCE (Before Common Era) the Bible was written over a period of 1500 years, by at least 40 authors from diverse backgrounds using three different languages from multiple locations across three continents. It includes literature genres ranging from poetry to prose to prophecy. Yet a consistent theme runs through it about God's redemption of humanity from the beginning of history until the end of the world and beyond. Bible scholar Craig Blomberg observes,

> The theological unity of Scripture, even amid all of its diversity, enables readers of all sixty-six books to discern a coherent narrative plot, profound wisdom, and a metanarrative that explains human nature from its origins to its final destiny. No other anthology of literature in the history of the world even attempts to undertake all three of these tasks simultaneously. The lives transformed for the better by the Bible's witness and the contributions to civilization that those people have made throughout history are disproportionately larger than in any other religion or ideology.[1]

Though we do not have the original texts, we have a very high level of confidence that the Bible we have today is the Bible that was written all those centuries ago. Take the New Testament for example. All 27 books were written in Greek during the first century CE (Common Era). Until now, archeologists have discovered and catalogued more than 5,000 Greek manuscripts, which are copies of the Scriptures. Some of those copies are from the second and third centuries. One is a complete copy of the New Testament books from 300 CE, a mere 200 years after the original authorship. Compare that with the next most copied ancient document, Homer's *Illiad*, of which there are about 650 manuscripts. The *Illiad* was written in about 800 BCE and the oldest copies archeologists have found are from the second and third century CE. That's about 1,000 years after it was written.[2] What that all means is the Bible is by far the best preserved ancient document in all of literature.

Naturally, not all the copies agree with every letter of all the other copies. They were all hand written and contain some copy errors. But with such a wealth of manuscripts, scholars are able to compare and contrast, using commonly accepted criteria, to identify which is most likely the original version. Many English translations have noted a few of these discrepancies in their footnotes. The vast majority of differences are simply spelling or very minor word variances.

Here is the amazing fact. Despite all the copy mistakes across centuries, "no orthodox doctrine or ethical practice of Christianity depends solely on any disputed wording."[3] In other words, all of the discrepancies between copies are minor and do not affect Christian doctrine. That is incredible. The core themes of the Bible's narrative survived not only the vast diversity of original authorship but also centuries of preservation. Theology professor Paul Enns concludes,

> There are no contradictions or inconsistencies within its pages. The Holy Spirit is the unifier of the sixty-six books, determining its harmonious consistency. In unity these books teach the triunity of God, the deity of Jesus Christ, the personality of the Holy Spirit, the fall and depravity of man, as well as salvation by grace. It quickly becomes apparent that no human being(s) could have orchestrated the harmony of the teachings of the Scripture. The divine authorship of the Bible is the only answer.[4]

What an awesome God!

The Bible is revelation.

Now that we know the Bible we have is accurate, let's take a step back and think about why we have the Bible at all. In short, the Bible is part of God's self-revelation to the world. Theologians talk about two kinds of revelation: General and Special.

General Revelation refers to everything that is created and can be observed by everyone in the world. The heavens and the earth and all that is in them point to God as a Creator. Flowing out of that observation, people from every generation have had a natural inclination to worship something that is greater than themselves. Something is ingrained in humans which drives them to give credit to something or someone else for the creation of the world. Beyond observing divine origins, each human has a natural sense of right and wrong. Of course, people sometimes disagree about what is wrong but everyone has a conscience that motivates them to reward what they perceive as right and punish those who do wrong. The Bible explains it like this,

> For what can be known about God is plain to them, because God has shown it to them. For his invisible attributes, namely, his eternal power and divine nature, have been clearly perceived, ever since the creation of the world, in the things that have been made. (Romans 1:19-20, ESV)

All this evidence, which is available to the whole world, is called General Revelation.

Special Revelation is the second kind of revelation. Special refers to the audience who receives this revelation, meaning only a particular set of people have seen or experienced this communication from God, specifically the person of Jesus Christ and the Bible. God was not content only to show people through nature that they were created. As a gracious and compassionate God, he also communicated with us his story of redemption, the plan to make things right and restore what has been broken. Simply put, the Bible is a product of God's mission. Bible scholar Christopher Wright explains it like this,

> The whole canon of Scripture is a missional phenomenon in the sense that it witnesses to the self-giving movement of this God toward his creation and us, human beings in God's own image, but wayward and

wanton. The writings that now comprise our Bible are themselves the product of and witness to the ultimate mission of God.[5]

God communicated with his people in order that they might know him.

The Bible is for the whole world.

You might be asking, if God only revealed Christ and the Bible to certain people what about the rest of humankind? How do they come to know Christ? In his sovereign plan, God gave to his people the task of sharing this Special Revelation with the rest of the world. Jesus told his disciples

> All authority in heaven and on earth has been given to me. Go therefore and make disciples of all nations, baptizing them in the name of the Father and of the Son and of the Holy Spirit, teaching them to observe all that I have commanded you. And behold, I am with you always, to the end of the age. (Matthew 28:18-20)

This command to share what Jesus taught has driven Christians for centuries to translate the Bible into local languages all over the world. For example, over the past five centuries, and especially since the early 20th century, English translations of the Bible have multiplied. There are dozens of translations, or versions, ranging from literal word for word translations like the New American Standard Bible (NASB) to a more dynamic, phrase by phrase effort like the New Living Translation (NLT). Both have strengths and weaknesses. The more literal versions ensure the reader has as close of access to the original text as possible without learning the original languages, but their English prose is stiff and sometimes hard to understand. The more dynamic translations still aim to be accurate to the original while communicating with common language so that the most people can understand the message. Other translations land somewhere in the middle, including the New International Version

(NIV) and the English Standard Version (ESV). A good piece of advice is to find one that you are comfortable reading and read the whole Bible in that version. Then when you do a more intense study of a particular section of the Bible it is helpful to compare versions to see how others have interpreted the original writing.

However, English is only one of more than 7,000 known languages in the world. While English has dozens of Bible translations, many people around the world do not have a single portion of the Bible in their local language, sometimes called "heart language." As of the year 2017, 650 languages have the full Bible, almost 2,600 have some portions of the Bible, and at least 1,600+ "are likely to need some form of Bible translation to begin."[6] This stark reality is a call to the Church to continue its efforts to spread the mission of God around the world, until the day John foresaw when

> a great multitude that no one could number, from every nation, from all tribes and peoples and languages, standing before the throne and before the Lamb, clothed in white robes, with palm branches in their hands, and crying out with a loud voice, "Salvation belongs to our God who sits on the throne, and to the Lamb!" (Revelation 7:9-10, ESV)

The Bible is the Word of God

As God's revelation to the world, the Bible not only contains the words of God, it is the Word of God. Besides the evidence from the miraculous collection and preservation of the Bible text over thousands of years, the Bible itself claims to be the Word of God. Hundreds of passages use phrases like "The Lord said…" For example,

> Now the Lord said to Abram, "Go from your country and your kindred and your father's house to the land that I will show you. And I will make of you a great nation, and I will bless you and make your name great, so that you will be a blessing. I will bless those who bless you, and him who

dishonors you I will curse, and in you all the families of the earth shall be blessed (Genesis 12:1-3)

This word and hundreds of others are clearly written to communicate a message from God.

Another bit of evidence that the Bible is God's Word is it claims to be given by God. "All Scripture is breathed out by God and profitable for teaching, for reproof, for correction, and for training in righteousness, that the man of God may be complete, equipped for every good work" (2 Timothy 3:16-17). This "breathing" of God means the Bible is not just a fancy idea made up by men and women, but the very words of God. He used each author's unique cultural background, temperament, and writing style to communicate exactly the message he wanted with language people could understand. They are truly his words.

As the Word of God, the Bible is truthful in all it intends to affirm. "It is impossible for God to lie" (Hebrews 6:18). "The words of the Lord are pure words, like silver refined in a furnace on the ground, purified seven times" (Psalm 12:6). God is truth and the standard by which everything true or false is determined. Yet as mentioned already, God chose to use humans to communicate his words. Their perspective of the world, such as "The sun rises, and the sun goes down, and hastens to the place where it rises" (Ecclesiastes 1:5), does not negate God's Word as true.[7] Rather it speaks in relatable language that reaches our hearts. Let us pray like Jesus did, "Sanctify them in the truth; your word is truth" (John 17:17).

Finally, if the Bible is the Word of God then it has authority over every part of our lives. To disobey the Word is to disobey God. To obey the Word of God is to gain life.

> Blessed is the man who walks not in the counsel of the wicked, nor stands in the way of sinners, nor sits in the seat of scoffers; but his delight is in

the law of the Lord, and on his law he meditates day and night. He is like a tree planted by streams of water" (Psalm 1:1-3, ESV)

Yet the authority of the Bible does not come from its rules which we as humans are obligated to follow. Rather it comes from the character and person of God and his acts of redemption, namely sending his Son to pay the penalty for our disobedience and make a way for new life through his resurrection.[8] Author Sally Lloyd-Jones puts it like this,

> Now, some people think the Bible is a book of rules, telling you what you should and shouldn't do. The Bible certainly does have some rules in it. They show you how life works best. But the Bible isn't mainly about you and what you should be doing. It's about God and what he has done.[9]

Conclusion

At the end of it all we can trust the Bible because it's God's written Word to you and to me, to generations past and generations future. It is the Word of hope and the Word of life, God's gracious revealing of himself and his plan of redemption for the whole world. May we delight in it and find blessing! For "the grass withers, the flower fades, but the word of our God will stand forever" (Isaiah 40:8, ESV).

DISCUSSION QUESTIONS

1. How does the Bible compare to other ancient literature?

2. How do you explain the difference between General Revelation and Special Revelation?

3. How does God intend to use the Bible in our lives - look at 2 Timothy 3:16-17?

Chapter 2

WHY IS THE BIBLE SO VIOLENT BUT JESUS IS SO LOVING?

Adam Embry

Why is the Bible so violent but Jesus is so loving? Great question, tough answer. But here's an attempt: The Bible, true to reality, describes both human violence and Jesus' love, and that love simultaneously judges our violence as sinful and vanquishes it. Let me unpack that answer.

The Bible is true to reality

The Bible describes reality, even its most violent, debased moments. Ancient near eastern cultures were marked by violence, tribal warfare, and the destruction of opposing nations and cultures. In that sense, the Bible doesn't describe anything out of the ordinary during its time. Based on the descriptions of Old Testament violence, atheist Richard Dawkins doesn't hold back in his assessment of Israel's God, Yahweh:

> "The God of the Old Testament is arguably the most unpleasant character in all fiction: jealous and proud of it; a petty, unjust, unforgiving control-freak; a vindictive, bloodthirsty ethnic cleanser; a misogynistic, homophobic, racist, infanticidal, genocidal, fili-malevolent bully. Those of us schooled from infancy in his ways can become desensitized to their horror."[1]

Dawkins is right that we can be desensitized. Here's the R-rated description of Old Testament violence:

> "Acts of reprobate violence explode from the pages of the Bible as evil people perform unspeakable acts. We read about children cannibalized (2 Kings 6:28-29; Ezek 5:10; Lam 2:20) and dashed against a rock (Ps 137:9). During the Babylonian invasion, Zedekiah is forced to watch his sons slaughtered, after which his own eyes are gouged out (Jer 52:10-11). Pregnant women are ripped open (2 Kings 15:16; Amos 1:13). Other women are raped (Gen 34:1-5; 1 Sam 13:1-15; Ezek 22:11); one of them is gang raped to the point of death (Judg 19:22-30). Military atrocities are equally shocking. We read about stabbings (Judg 3:12-20; 2 Sam 2:23; 20:10) and beheadings (1 Sam 17:54; 2 Sam 4:7-9). These are normal military atrocities. More extraordinary cases involve torture and mutilation: limbs are cut off (Judg 1:6-7), bodies hewed in pieces (1 Sam 15:33), eyes gouged out (Judg 16:21; 2 Kings 25:7), skulls punctured (Judg 4:12-23; 5:26-27) or crushed by a millstone pushed from a city wall (Judg 9:53). Two hundred foreskins are collected (1 Sam 18:27), seventy heads gathered (2 Kings 10:7-8), thirty men killed for their clothing (Judg 14:19). Bodies are hanged (Josh 8:29), mutilated and displayed as trophies (1 Sam 31:9-10), trampled beyond recognition (2 Kings 9:30-37), destroyed by wild beasts (Josh 13:8; 2 Kings 2:23-24) or flailed with briers (Judg 8:16). Entire groups are massacred (1 Sam 22:18-19; 1 Kings 16:8-14) or led into captivity strung together with hooks through their lips (Amos 4:2)."[2]

The list is worth reading, because it reminds us of our human depravity. The Bible doesn't deny the sinfulness of the human condition. It affirms we are sinfully violent. But the Bible doesn't recommend violence.

The atheist Christopher Hitchens thinks the Old Testament doesn't address the solution for violence when he asks, "Is it too modern to notice that there is nothing about the protection of children from cruelty, nothing about rape, nothing about slavery, and nothing about genocide [in the Old Testament]?"[3] No, it's not too modern to notice, and none of these issues didn't go unnoticed in biblical times.

The Bible says nothing about the violence of child cruelty? Surely Hitchens knows this, but in contrast to other nations, Israel was forbidden to offer child sacrifices to idols (Leviticus 18:21; 20:3; Deuteronomy 12:30-31; 18:10; Psalm 106:37). It's just not true that there was nothing about the protection of children from cruelty. As Psalm 127:3 affirms, "Children are a heritage from the Lord."

The Bible says nothing about the violence of rape?

The sexual ethic of the Old Testament was faithful, loving monogamy between husband and wife, a male and female, as defined in Genesis 2:24, which is the basis for the command not to commit adultery in Exodus 20:14. In fact, an entire book of the Old Testament, the Song of Songs, is a love story explaining to us the beauty of husband and wife being naked and not ashamed. For this reason, rape and any sort of sexual violence, including having multiple wives, doesn't go unnoticed in the biblical narrative.[4] From the rape of Tamar in Genesis 38 to the rape and murder of a Levite's whore in Judges 19, rape is condemned not by a specific command – "thou shalt not rape" – but through the fateful and horrific consequences of the sin that violate God's standard for sexual morality.[5]

The Bible says nothing about the violence of slavery?

It's key to remember that the nation of Israel and the churches throughout the Roman empire didn't invent slavery. In the fallen state of humanity, God determined that in Israel slavery had to be regulated for a temporary time of six years (Exodus 21:2; Deuteronomy 15:12, 18). Israel was forbidden to kill slaves (Exodus 21:20; Leviticus 24:17, 22) and had to treat them justly, since they bear God's name (Leviticus 25:43-55). And unlike later Greek and Roman cultures, slavery in the Ancient Near East wasn't based on slave-labor. Later in the first century, Christian slaves held equal status with non-slaves in the church (1 Corinthians 7:22; Galatians 3:28). The New Testament rejects the idea of selling humans into slavery (Acts 16:16-24; Colossians 4:1; Ephesians 6:9; 1 Timothy 1:9-11). And in more recent times when discussions of modern slavery arise, it's good to remember that, "During the 1790s and early 1880s the framework of evangelical theology and spirituality gave a significant ideological impetus to anti-slavery on both sides of the Atlantic," most specifically seen in the end of British slave trade in 1807 and the British emancipation act in 1833, both driven by Christian evangelical efforts.[6] Without the Judeo-Christian ethic of the image of God and human freedom, the British empire wouldn't have ended slavery. Just saying.

A few words need to be said about Israel's conquest of Canaan and other times when entire cities and civilizations were destroyed. The violence was brutal, a "complete destruction" of men, women, children, and animals (Genesis 19:29; Numbers 21:2-3; Deuteronomy 20:17; Joshua 6:17, 21; 1 Samuel 15). So, then, wasn't the God of the Old Testament for genocide? No. Rather, God was for the destruction of the violent, and he gave them time to repent. Four hundred years, to be exact (Genesis 15:13-14). The pagans in the land of Canaan practiced child molestation and sacrifice, incest, temple prostitution, adultery, homosexuality, and bestiality.[7] It was no innocent culture that God judged.

The Bible doesn't silence #metoo moments. It exposes violence and judges it as sinful. As civilizations turned their hearts to violence, God turned to judgment (Genesis 6:5-7). Laws for Israel throughout

Exodus, Leviticus, and Deuteronomy were enacted to protect victims, but the law couldn't change hardened hearts. God ended episodes of violence and saved his people by judging the wicked. Jim Hamilton explains the relationship between salvation and judgment:

> "Salvation always comes through judgment. Salvation for the nation of Israel at the Exodus came through the judgment of Egypt, and this pattern is repeated throughout the Old Testament, becoming paradigmatic even into the New. When God saves his people, he delivers them by bringing judgment on their enemies."[8]

The pattern of God saving his people and judging the wicked occurred in "each major redemptive event in the Bible – the fall, flood, exodus, exile from the land, the death and resurrection of Jesus, and the return of Christ."[9] When Adam and Eve sin, God judged the earth and the couple, but promised salvation and rescue from Satan. When violence later overtook the earth, God judged by sending a flood and saving Noah's family. When the Egyptians persecuted Israel, God judged Egypt through plagues and saved Israel by taking them through the Red Sea and drowning Pharaoh and his army. When Israel became a violent, idolatrous aggressor to the nations, God judged them by sending them into exile in foreign lands but saved an obedient remnant who returned to the land in peace. The scope of the Old Testament was marked by God's judgment on violent nations, including Israel. But he also saved his people from violence. He didn't ignore their cries for help (Exodus 2:23; 3:9; Nehemiah 1:5-6). He came to save, and he ultimately did so in Jesus.

The Bible is True to Jesus' Love

Jesus loved me and gave himself for me (Galatians 2:20). There's no truth greater that can calm a violent heart. Jesus loved me. Slowly read over those words. Truth: I am loved. But how? He knows the coworker we hate. The man or woman we lust after. The moments we glare spitefully at our children. The moments of self-violence, self-harm, our self-destructive idolatry. The moments we don't like God. No, hate him. And yet he loves us! His love comes to us when we are unlovable and have no love for him. God shows his love for us," Paul says in Romans 5:8, "in that while we were still sinners Christ died for us." While we were still sinners. While all the crud was in our hearts. Divine love moving towards violent people, overtaking us, tracking us down. Love loving the unlovable. Love softening a hard-heart. Love winning. Love defeating our violence.

Jesus' Love & Our Violence

Jesus loves me, this I know, for the Bible tells me so. What a simple truth from a simple children's song. Here's what's also true: what Jesus knew when he read his Bible was that his Father loved him – and us – for his Bible told him so. Jesus' Bible was the Old Testament, filled with acts of violence and judgment. Jesus didn't shy away from identifying himself with the God of the Old Testament, his Father. The real conundrum isn't that the Bible is so violent but Jesus is so loving. It's that Jesus loves the God of the Old Testament and calls him his Father.

Why is the connection between the Father's and Son's love important? Because flowing out of the Father's love for Jesus is Jesus' love for us, a love that was willing to endure a violent death to rid us of our violence so we can love others. Read over parts of John 15:9-17 below.

> As the Father has loved me, so have I loved you. Abide in my love. If you keep my commandments, you will abide in my love, just as I have kept my Father's commandments and abide in his love. These things I have spoken to you, that my joy may be in you, and that your joy may be full. This is my commandment, that you love one another as I have loved you. Greater love has no one than this, that someone lay down his life for his

friends. . . .These things I command you, so that you will love one another.

Jesus loves us, and yet his death for us judges our violence as worthy of punishment. He gave himself for us (Galatians 2:20). Christ died for the ungodly (Romans 5:6). He bore our sins in his body on the tree (1 Peter 2:24). He was the sacrificial lamb that was slain (Revelation 5:12). Pierced in his hands and feet for our transgressions (Isaiah 53:5). The violence inflicted against Jesus on the cross was what we deserved. Yet he took our place, so we might have peace and healing (Isaiah 53:5).

Does the Cross Condone Violence?

But there's a serious objection to consider. Is the cross just a murderous exchange of a sinless life for a sinful one, just a perverted way to end violence? No, because Jesus' violent death on the cross is more than a legal exchange of his sinless life in the place of ours. His death provides so much more than forgiveness of sins. Yes, his death is an exchange of his righteousness for our unrighteousness. But God returns our violence with greater love. It's not an even exchange. He gives to us more than he takes away in removing our sin. He gives us the gift of the Spirit, deliverance from spiritual bondage to Satan and idolatry, provides entrance into a new covenant and creation, and peace with God and others.[10]

Conclusion

The Bible, true to reality, describes both human violence and Jesus' love, and that love simultaneously judges our violence as sinful and vanquishes it. There's no better way to round out this chapter than letting John Webster explain what happened on that violent cross so many years ago:

If we're not careful, we can think that what's happening in the passion [Jesus' suffering] is that God is simply punishing an innocent victim for our wrongdoings – as if God simply requires that the punishment for our crimes should be enacted, and it doesn't matter who is punished. But Jesus is not just a mute sacrificial animal. If he is like a lamb led to the slaughter, it's not because God is victimizing him; it is because he is God himself fulfilling his own purpose; it is because he is God the Son, freely and loving acting out the will of the Father. . . That does not mean that God just vented his anger at sin on Jesus. It means that he, Jesus, the Son of God, is God himself bearing the wounds of our wickedness. God does not save us by sacrificing someone other than himself. God sacrifices himself. In his Son, God himself bears our sins. . . as Colossians puts it, 'in him' – Jesus – 'all the fulness of God was pleased to dwell, and through him to reconcile to himself all things, whether on earth or in heaven, making peace by the blood of his cross (Colossians 1:19)[11]

Jesus' lavish love vanquishes our violence.

DISCUSSION QUESTIONS

1. What does it mean that Christ died for us while we were still sinners? How does that impact our view of non-believers around us?

2. How can we, as Christians, not brush over Old Testament violence, but also explain the bigger picture & story of the Bible?

3. How does the Old Testament violence, God's judgement, and Christ's love impact the way we see violence & injustice in the world today?

Chapter 3

IS JESUS REALLY THE ONLY WAY TO BE SAVED?

Garrett Wishall

In January 2012, my wife and I moved with our family — two boys at the time — to Denver, Colorado. We were coming from the midwest: the land of churches; the land of hardworking folks; the Bible Belt. We knew things would be different in Denver, one of the lowest-ranked states for religious affiliation and church attendance.[1] We expected opposition to the gospel, maybe even antagonism. Instead, what we got was tolerance.

> "What's good for you is good for you; what's good for me is good for me."

This mantra rules the day in Denver and many places around the world. If you share the gospel, people will usually politely listen and then tell you how for them, exercise, yoga or spending a lot of time outdoors is the ticket. That's what "makes them happy." People are kind enough. They give you a nod on the street, briefly converse on a hiking trail, wave from their driveway and then continue on their way. The more proactive and passionate ones will try to persuade you about why you should be vegan or try another specific diet, but for the most part "what's good for you is good for you; what's good for me is good for me." Tolerance is pervasive in our city and I suspect in yours as well.

Is that a problem?

So, what about tolerance? Is it biblical? Particularly when it comes to questions of eternity, how one gets to God, or how you can be saved. Should we tolerate different viewpoints on religious and spiritual matters, believing that there while they are many different paths, they all ultimately lead to God? Or at least if you have a sincere religion with a God, then you are probably good? Must we believe and proclaim that only belief in Jesus saves?

Christians throughout history hold to the truth that Jesus is the only way you can be saved, and we proclaim this in our churches. With excitement we proclaim it! We seek to make Jesus known in our churches and throughout the world. To briefly explain why we think only belief in Jesus saves, we need to look at the authority of Scripture, the truth that everyone needs a Savior and how Jesus is that Savior.

The Authority of Scripture

We believe there is one God and that he has revealed himself in Scripture. We believe Scripture is the verbal, complete and inspired Word of God. We believe Scripture is without error in its original manuscripts, supernaturally superintended through translation and accurate in everything it addresses. As such, we believe Scripture possesses infallible divine authority on all matters on which it touches.

The Chicago Statement on Biblical Inerrancy speaks to the danger of deviating from the *authority* of Scripture:

> The authority of Scripture is inescapably impaired if this total divine inerrancy is in any way limited or disregarded, or *made relative to a view of truth contrary to the Bible's own*; and such lapses bring serious loss to both the individual and the Church (emphasis mine).[2]

In this age of tolerance, making authoritative truth claims is not in vogue. If you say you believe truth is objective, not subjective, you might get a funny look. If you say there is one God and he has revealed himself in one authoritative book you will likely get a look that says, "What did you say? What a crazy, inappropriate statement!" Intolerance is maybe the chief social misstep of our day, viewed as unloving and unhelpful. But allowing someone to go down a path of error in the name of tolerance is actually the unhelpful and unloving act. If we believe we hold in our hands the inspired Word of God, we must learn its message, submit to it, embrace it and share it with others.[3]

"Okay," you might say, "Great, Scripture is authoritative. So, what does it talk about? Does it address matters of salvation, how one is saved, and if there are multiple ways to God?" It does. As seen in the Baptist Faith and Message 2000, Scripture has salvation for its end and is a testimony to Jesus Christ, who is himself the focus of divine revelation.[4] That is, God gave Scripture as a revelation of himself, that we might know him and live in eternal relationship with him. So, what does Scripture say about matters of salvation?

Everyone needs a Savior.

Scripture teaches that God made the world (Genesis 1-2). In seven days, God made the world and everything in it. He created by the power of his word, speaking into existence things that did not exist (Hebrews 11:3). This is called creation *ex nihilo*, out of nothing. And all of God's creation was good (Genesis 1).

Scripture also teaches that creation provides evidence of a Creator. Because of the created order, every person in every country of the world knows that God exists (Romans 1:20). Because every person knows there is a Creator, they also know that they should submit to this Creator, that they are not him, and that they should live their lives under the Creator, according to his Word. But they don't. Instead of submitting to him, they go their own way and steal the glory and honor that is rightfully his (Romans 1:21; Isaiah 53:6). They follow their own desires, their own paths and live as if they are their own god.

This mutiny against the Creator began in the Garden of Eden at the beginning of time. Scripture teaches that the apex of God's creation was man. Created male and female, man bears the image of God (Genesis 1:26-28). We can think and reason as he does, we possess similar traits — for example the ability to love and show kindness — and we have moral capacity. In addition to having moral capacity, God made man with relational capacity just as God has relational capacity within himself — he exists eternally as one God and three persons, Father, Son and Holy Spirit. Man's relational capacity includes the ability to have relationship with God and in the beginning the first man and woman, Adam and Eve, had perfect relationship with God. Until the Fall.

Genesis 3 records the account of Adam and Eve sinning against God. Satan — a fallen angel who is God's enemy — took the form of a serpent and led them astray. Adam and Eve went against God's command to not eat fruit from the tree of the knowledge of good and evil, choosing to be god themselves instead of submitting to God and glorifying him. Romans 5 and Ephesians 2 teach that every person after Adam has been born dead in sin, by nature and by choice. We follow in the way of our predecessor, failing to honor God as God (Romans 1:21). Scripture is clear that the penalty for our sin is death (Romans 6:23) and after death eternal separation from God. Unless. Unless God provides a way to be saved.

In the very chapter where the first sin took place, sin that demands punishment, God spoke of a remedy. Genesis 3:15 says that a future offspring of Adam would crush the head of the serpent. The rest of the first 39 books of the Bible known as the Old Testament details the formation and movement of God's people. Leader after leader arises to lead God's people, only to one day die. None of them live forever, a requirement to be the one who crushes the serpent, for his chief weapon is death. God creates a sacrificial system to "cover" the sins of the people, just as he covered Adam and Eve's nakedness in the garden. But always with these countless animal offerings was an awareness that an eternal remedy was needed. The people looked and longed for God's salvation, for the One who would come and save his people.

Jesus is the Savior.

The first four books of the New Testament detail the coming of that Savior. They begin with the birth of a boy. Not just any boy and not just any birth, but Jesus Christ — the Son of God — miraculously conceived by God the Spirit in the womb of a virgin named Mary (Matt 1:18-20). Matthew 1:21 tells us what Jesus came to do, "She will bear a son, and you shall call his name Jesus, for he will save his people from their sins." Here was the long-anticipated Savior! The Gospels tell the story of Jesus' perfect life. He lived without fault and error, always honoring God and giving him glory. Jesus obeyed God in every instance, every situation. This qualified him to be the way to God. To be the One who could open the door to restored relationship with God. But more had to happen before this could take place.

After his perfect life, Jesus died. He was crucified in shame on a Roman cross by men who were blinded by hatred and personal ambition. But this was not the end. Three days after he died, Jesus rose from the grave. He again walked the earth, visiting his disciples, before ascending to heaven to sit and reign at God's right hand. In his person and work, Jesus thus crushed Satan. Sin demands punishment and Jesus took the punishment in his death on the cross. And Jesus then rose from the dead, conquering sin and death and squelching Satan's power (Hebrews 2:14-15).

The Way, the Truth and the Life

Through his perfect life, death and resurrection Jesus himself became the way to God. Romans 10:9-10 explain how this takes place:

> "because, if you confess with your mouth that Jesus is Lord and believe in your heart that God raised him from the dead, you will be saved. For with the heart one believes and is justified, and with the mouth one confesses and is saved."

This is how salvation takes place. This is the way back to God. In Acts 4:12 Peter says, "there is salvation in no one else, for there is no other name under heaven given among men by which we must be saved." In John 14:6 Jesus says, "I am the Way, and the Truth, and the Life. No one comes to the Father except through me." 1 Timothy 2:5 says, "For there is one God, and there is one mediator between God and men, the man Christ Jesus." Chapters 7-9 in Hebrews describe the qualifications necessary to be the Savior, including perfection (7:28), an unending life (7:25) and entering God's holy presence through one's own personal holiness (9:12). Philippians 2:10-11 says that one day every knee will bow at the name of Jesus, confessing him as Lord. Finally, the book of

Revelation describes the second coming of Jesus and how all those who believe in him will go to an eternity in his Kingdom and all those who reject him to an eternal hell. We thus know that belief in Jesus is the only way to God both because the whole storyline of Scripture and multiple specific references within Scripture say so.

The mantra, "what's good for you, is good for you and what's good for me is good for me" might be true when it comes to choosing your sports teams or favorites foods. But when it comes to matters of salvation and how one is saved, we can accept only one view. Jesus is the way to God the Father, the way to be saved, the way to eternal joy. May the name of Jesus be on our lips as he is the only way to God.

DISCUSSION QUESTIONS

1. How would you describe the spiritual climate around you in terms of how people view Jesus?

2. How does the Bible teach that Jesus is the only way for salvation?

3. How can you begin to share about Jesus's salvation to someone who doesn't share the same views as you?

Chapter 4

HOW CAN I COMPREHEND THAT GOD IS THREE-IN-ONE?

Franck Corbiere

> Prayer to the Triune God: Heavenly Father, blessed Son, eternal Spirit, I adore Thee as one Being, one Essence, one God in three distinct Persons, for bringing sinners to Thy knowledge and to Thy kingdom. [1]
> —*The Valley of Vision*

> The grace of the Lord Jesus Christ, and the love of God and the fellowship of the Holy Spirit be with you all (2 Corinthians 13:14).

Have you ever asked a Muslim friend what he thought of the Trinity? The common response shared by those who believe in Islam would be that the Christian faith engages itself in nonsense because of its claim that God is one in three, and three in one. Have you ever met a Jehovah Witness at your doorstep, and asked them what they think of the doctrine of the Trinity? They would answer that this is a doctrine worthy of the Middle-Ages, which was created during that era, and that it is an absurd idea taught by old men with grey hair in theological schools. For them, God is a unique and eternal Being, who does not need to be made known and has no equal to him, and someone who revealed Jehovah has never existed. Perhaps you think of your Mormon neighbors.

Have you discussed with them what the Bible teaches about the Triune God? How do you think they will respond? "Well,..." they will say, "Adam is our father and our God, and the only God with whom we are dealing. God was once similar to the human race, and actually was a divine man. God is not spirit, but a man like Brigham Young." I can go on and on mentioning diverse beliefs that reject the biblical truth about the Trinity but, there can only be one truth and the others have to be wrong. This eternal truth is revealed in the Scripture. As a Christian, do you thoroughly comprehend the nature and purpose of the Trinity the way the Bible displays it in its theological context? Are you confused by it and do you not know how to articulate this amazing biblical doctrine? I pray that these few pages will help you grow in your knowledge and understanding of the Trinity.

How can I simultaneously comprehend the unity of God and God three-in-one?

Biblical Christianity rooted in its historicity, and born from the Scripture, simply teaches monotheism, and describes the Godhead as three persons who are united into one unique and only God. It is one of the great truths of the Old Testament: "Hear O Israel! The Lord is our God, The Lord is **one**!"[2] The same truth is also taught in the New Testament, for instance in Galatians 3:20, "Now an intermediary implies more than one, but God is **one**." Jesus himself acknowledges the monotheist belief in Mark 12:29, and this is unanimous among Christ's early disciples in 1 Corinthians 8:6 and James 2:19. The Bible affirms that, "God's divine nature is undivided and indivisible".[3] This means that God does not consist of parts nor can he be divided into parts. God's being is unique, and needs to be understood in a simple manner as one essence, absent of any composed distinct units, because God is spirit and is not inclined to any such division, unlike a human's nature which is composed of material and immaterial parts.

Now the difficulty for us in understanding, is that this unity is not inconsistent with the conception of the Triune God. Thiessen interestingly points out:

> The unity of God allows for the existence of personal distinctions in the divine nature, while at the same time recognizing that the divine nature is numerically and eternally one. Unity does imply that the three persons of the Trinity are not separate essences within the divine essence.[4]

A reasonable mind can easily make the case for the unity of God, but the biblical doctrine of the Trinity comes to us from direct divine revelation in human terms, from God's Word. It has been transmitted by the preaching of His Word by prophets, priests, kings and teachers of the Old and New Testament era.

Everyone knows that the term "Trinity" is not found in the Scripture, however it did have an early usage in the church, and clearly Trinitarian faith and thinking are present throughout the pages of the Bible. Τριας (*trias*) is the Greek form that seems to be first mentioned by Theophilus of Antioch in A.D. 181, and the Latin word, *trinita* ("threeness"), was then employed by Tertullian in A.D. 220. The historical Christian doctrine of the Trinity that the early Church fathers fought for, defined it as three eternal persons in the one divine essence, known as Father: the "fountain of deity", Son: the eternal only begetting one (*monogenes*), and Holy Spirit: the sent One. About these three distinct persons, one may speak of the "hypostasis for the plurality of God."[5] Thus John Frame goes a little bit further by saying:

> Person is simply a label for the ways in which the Father, Son and Spirit are alike, in distinction from the Godhead as a whole.[6]

The important Athanasian Creed affirms the Trinitarian Christian belief, and its worship to the Triune God:

> We worship one God in the Trinity, and the Trinity in unity; we distinguished among the persons, but we do not divide the substance... The entire three persons are coeternal and coequal with one another... we worship complete unity in Trinity and Trinity in unity.[7]

Why is it so important to believe in the Trinity and know how to explain it?

It is an important pillar of the Christian faith, for which the early Church Fathers were ready to die. They spent a lot of time speaking at length about this doctrine and wrote creeds about it so that this biblical truth wouldn't lose its impetus for the next generation of believers. God was successful to preserve through the ages, the doctrine of the Trinity, mainly through the ordinance of baptism. When Jesus ordained baptism to the disciples, "in the name *(NOTE: in the singular, signifying one God)* of the Father and of the Son and of the Holy Spirit." Therefore, in this account we are face to face with three persons who are the ONE God to whom Christians commit their lives as disciples (Matthew 28:19). The theologian John Frame refers to this as the "economic" Trinity,[8] and how each member of the Godhead relates to each other in Creation. We can apply the same principle to Jesus' baptism in Mark 1:9-11: the Father deferred to the Son, and the Holy Spirit revealed his presence in the Son's life and ministry. As we also read the Trinitarian blessing in 2 Corinthians 13:14 prayed by Paul, that the grace of Christ Jesus, the love of the Father and the communion that we have with each believer in the presence of the Holy Spirit being in us, we can see that it testifies of our personal and corporate relationship to the Triune God. The many biblical references of the Triune God are striking examples that should remind us that the

New Testament is plain and clear on that doctrine, although never explicit in the Old Testament.

The New City Catechism answers the self-evident question: "How many persons are there in God?" It responds that:

> There are three persons in the one true and living God: The Father, the Son, and the Holy Spirit. They are the same in substance, equal in power and glory.[9]

The last portion of the answer speaks of the ontological Trinity, in that there is "no subordination among the persons."[10] This means that when we say the Father, the Son and the Spirit are "the same in substance and equal," it affirms that they are equally God, and thus equally divine. Therefore, the three personal "subsistences," from the Greek "Hypostasis," speak of the eternal existence, reality and the constitutionality of the equality of the divine persons in the Godhead. Each one of them are self-aware, each being "I" (or ego) in relation to the two other persons, and each sharing the full essence of the deity. It is important not to confuse this with *modalism*, which describes God as three persons, each one playing their roles by wearing their mask, and thus, each one revealing God and his way, which they take on in human history. We are also not talking about *tritheism*, which portrays three gods as a crew engaged in a divine task. Both of those theories are heresy. In plain words, we are referring to one God (gender: He), and that God is likewise "they," who are eternally cohabiting, co-working, co-engaging where the Father, initiates his eternal plan, the Only Son, fulfills the plan, and the Holy Spirit, executes the plan by yielding to the will of both, which is also his will.

Finally, if we believe as Christians that the words of Jesus are truth, and his works revealed that truth about God, and they support the reality of our salvation as the New Testament sets forth, then we have the confidence in the Lord and the responsibility to give equal honor and worship to all three members of the Triune God in their unity of merciful and gracious ministry towards us. This is the gospel revealing the Trinity of which Jesus had an evangelistic conversation with Nicodemus in the garden of Gethsemane in John 3. That should give us joy in our heart and fill us with thanksgiving to God to intimately commune with God the Father, God the Son and God the Spirit. We know by faith that God has made his home in us, and his glory comes down by his grace. Each day should be a day of being fully grateful to the Triune God. I will finish with these words from the theologian Eric Mascall, about this inseparable union among the three persons in the Godhead as he states that it,

> is the secret of God's most infinite life and being, into which, in His infinite love and generosity, He has admitted us, and is therefore to be accepted with amazed and exultant gratitude.[11]

I pray that we may be in constant fellowship with each person of the Trinity, and through this we may find full joy, have an unspeakable amazement and be eternally thankful for the deep mystery of the Triune God!

DISCUSSION QUESTIONS

1. To what extent does the Bible teach the doctrine of the Trinity?

2. How would you explain the view of Triune God in your own words?

3. What are the views that are different from the doctrine of the Trinity? And how can you distinguish them?

part two

HONEST QUESTIONS ABOUT...
GOD'S CHURCH

Chapter 5

CAN I LOVE JESUS BUT NOT THE CHURCH?

Michael Morgan

Jesus is amazing.

The person and work of Jesus is so compelling, he is so ridiculously wonderful, that it bewilders me time and again whenever I hear about people walking away from him. Jesus is the greatest there ever was: He's the source and sum of all that's good. If every star in the sky could be gathered into one massive orb, he would outshine them all by the radiance of his beauty. If all the money in all the world were collected into one heaping pile, the riches of his majesty would make it look like a pittance.

Everything about him is amazing. His love extends to the heavens, his faithfulness to the clouds. He cares for the weak and looks after the lowly. His heart is full of compassion. The Bible tells us that a bruised reed he will not break, and a faintly burning wick, he will not put out. In other words, he's not going to kick you while you're down. Jesus is a friend of sinners: failures and liars and prostitutes. He lifts up those who've fallen. He pulls close those who've been cast out. He restores the broken, heals the hurting, loves the unlovely. This dude walked on water and stilled the sea and stood up to self-righteous Pharisees.

This is One whom I could follow.

He's perfect in every way. He went to the cross on our behalf and took care of sin, once and for all. He rose again, defeating sin, Satan, death, and hell. No wonder we stand in awe, no wonder we love this One who in grace has set His love on us. Jesus is simply amazing.

His followers, on the other hand? Not so much.

A hard look in the mirror tells me all I need to know: I can be petty and prideful, hypocritical and gossipy, lazy and mean and unforgiving, self-righteous, cliquish, angry and overbearing. Throw me in a pot, along with a bunch of other sinners whom Jesus loves, add water, and stir. That's the church.

For many of us, the idea of forfeiting the one day of the week that we could sleep in so that we can spend it with a bunch of strangers sounds about as fun as sand in your underpants or licking a bug zapper. Yet it gets even better: the Bible calls us to give, not one morning a week to these awkward people, but our very lives. No surprise people are asking the question, "Can I love Jesus, but <u>not</u> the church?"[1] After all, we've heard legends of blue-haired widows fighting over whose casserole contribution to the pot-luck was better, how deacon boards have split the church over a decision concerning carpet colors, or how the old pastor ran off with the secretary. Whether any of it's true or not, why would we want to associate ourselves with a group of people notoriously behind the times, obviously pock-marked, and decidedly not-cool?

Why? In short, because we cannot truly love Jesus without *also* loving his church. It is impossible.

Loving Jesus isn't theoretical.

Loving people in the church pushes our love for Jesus from theory to reality. 1 John 4:20 always makes me squirm: "If anyone says, 'I love God,' and hates his brother, he is a liar; for he who does not love his brother whom he has seen cannot love God whom he has not seen." It is easier to claim Christ than it is to claim his people. Yet Jesus loves us so much that he won't allow us to walk through life self-deluded, thinking that we know and love God, if in truth, we don't. The church is the playground where real love is worked out. It is in real life interactions with real people that we learn how to truly and genuinely love.

It is easy for me to convince myself of my deep love for Jesus. After all, I relish quiet mornings in rented cabins, a hot cup of coffee in hand, the kids playing happily outside, while I journal and read the Psalms. I enjoy Christian music, and as I dart through traffic, I hum the words, and think nice thoughts—it's "positive and encouraging," after all. And I do love other Christians—at least some of them—you know, those that I "connect" with—those that have similar interests, similar tastes. Those who act like me, and think like me, and look like me, and smell like me—man, I love those people. Or do I?

Maybe I just love myself.

It is easy to convince ourselves that we truly love Jesus, even though in our hearts, we despise certain people around us. 1 John 4:20 calls that out for what it is: a false love. A mirage, a cheap, knock-off version of the real thing.

As my favorite author once wrote:

> To love the church is to love the whole church. Beggars, addicts, womanizers, cougars, yuppies, snotty children, the old, the irrelevant, the stupid, the ugly, the materialistic, moralistic, opportunistic, the selfish, the arrogant, the cheaters, the liars, the holier-than-thous. There is no escaping. To say otherwise is to say that you are better, holier, closer to

God. Are you closer to the One who suffered and died for them? Then you will die, too. Most likely your 'suffering' will be putting up with them, your dying will be to yourself. But it's the only way.[2]

Why is it, in John 17, when Jesus prays for all future believers, that unity is given the place of priority? Because this is where love is worked out. Honestly, it's often easier to love people who don't follow Christ than it is to love others in the church. I look at another Christian, and think, "They ought to know better." I seem to have a lower tolerance for others within the Body of Christ than I do for those who don't follow Jesus. It is easier to love those who are distant than those who are close, because when you get close to someone, you start to notice all the things that are wrong with them. All their flaws get magnified, all their warts are out in the open, all their junk now affects you.

Think about dating and marriage. A new couple falls in love—the guy was "taken at once" with the girl across the room, and the new couple bat their eyes at each other, hearts all aflutter, pitter-pat! Fast forward a decade: lots of unseen faults are now front and center. Now they can't stand each other; all they do is bicker and tear one another down. It's painless to love imaginary people. It's not difficult to feel fondly toward those with whom we have never truly had to deal. But it's something else altogether when you're rubbing shoulders all the time.

I'll never forget flying back to the United States from Hong Kong. It was a fourteen-hour flight, and I was seated next to a guy who had not mastered the concept of personal space. He hogged the arm rest the whole time, leaned on me, and kept rubbing his arm against mine. Thirty minutes into the flight, I was a little tired of it. A couple hours later, and I'm pretty annoyed. After about five hours, I began trying, with my shoulder, to shove him back into his seat. By the eight-hour mark, I had developed a permanent twitch. Before we landed, I was just praying that I wouldn't kill somebody. The whole time, my inside voice was at top volume: "He's in my space! Get out of my space!" You could say that we were up close and personal.

This is the place where we learn to love; this is the place where Jesus prays for us to be one. Right there, up close, rubbing shoulders, in each other's personal space: "Love people there," Jesus says. "If you have learned to love there, perhaps you have truly loved Me." It is in those close spaces that we become more like Jesus. It's in our rubbing up against others, our frequent and honest interactions, that we rub off our sharp edges. It's there that we learn to both extend and receive grace. It's there that love for Jesus moves from a simple platitude to genuine expression.

In John 14:15, Jesus reminded his disciples: "If you love me, you will keep my commandments." Curiously enough, this was immediately on the heels of John 13:34, where Jesus had just told them, "A new commandment I give to you, that you love one another; just as I have loved you, you also are to love one another." As others have said, it's hard to be close to the Shepherd when we refuse to get close to other sheep.

Loving What He Loves

Loving the church isn't always a grind, as it were. His love for us is transformative, not coercive. As we walk with Jesus, he transforms us, and he changes our affections to reflect his own. Our Savior is not after simple compliance, but the heartfelt devotion of the Psalmist: "I find my delight in your commandments, which I love" (Psalm 119:47). If we love Jesus, we will find ourselves also loving the things that he loves, namely, the church. After all, the church is Christ's bride. Anyone who has seen their friends married off has experienced one of two things. After the wedding, we either form a new friendship with the spouse, while deepening the relationship that was already present, or for whatever reason, we don't, and the friendship that we once enjoyed fades over time. It really is that simple.

We must not think of the church as though she were a little thing to God; some hobby on the side, some annoying infatuation, a fad that Jesus will outgrow in time.

> Christ loved the church and gave himself up for her, that he might sanctify her, having cleansed her by the washing of water with the word, so that he might present the church to himself in splendor, without spot or wrinkle or any such thing, that she might be holy and without blemish (Ephesians 5:25-27)

All of history is marching toward the great wedding feast of the risen Lamb!

You may find that you can enjoy deep friendship with someone despite the fact that you hold very different ideas about sports, politics, or even religion. However, you're unlikely to experience much intimacy with someone who deeply loves their spouse, while knowing full well that you're not a fan. Can you love Jesus, but not the church? Hardly; our love for Christ's bride will swell in parallel fashion to our growing love of Christ himself, if it is indeed genuine. In other words, our maturity in Christ is betrayed by our love for the church. Further, since loving Jesus is not theoretical, it is not enough to say, "I love *the* church," without also being able to say, "I love *this* church." For only love applied is love actual. Rick Warren said it best in his response to those who would claim membership only in the invisible church: "When you are sick, will your invisible pastor visit you?"[3] How about your invisible brothers or your imaginary mentor? The casualty of rejecting structure, heirarchy, or organization is often Christian community. "Little children, let us not love in word or talk but in deed and in truth" (1 John 3:18).

Loving with His Love

The love that we as Christians experience is a Trinitarian love, a love that's on the move. As "the Father is the lover and head of the Son, so the Son goes out to be the lover and head of the church."[4] Therefore, our love for Jesus must not be stagnant. The great love that the Son has shown his church must continue to flow outward, that God's glory would be known to the ends of the earth. The church, after all, is his chosen vehicle to accomplish his mission in the world. It may be an old truck that sputters, has some rust, isn't very fuel efficient, and clearly needs a tune up, but it's God's, he dearly loves it, and He's chosen to use it to deliver the best news ever. If you want to go for the ride, you need to get in. According to Jesus, our love for each other is a compelling witness to a dying world:

> I do not ask for these only, but also for those who will believe in me through their word, that they may all be one, just as you, Father, are in me, and I in you, that they also may be in us, so that the world may believe that you have sent me." (John 17:20-21)

As the old spiritual goes, "they will know we are Christians by our love, by our love."

If you love Jesus, you'll love his bride, no matter how many warts she may have. Loving the church is not to ignore her faults, but it must be more than simply standing around critiquing them. Instead, we've been called to humbly count others as more significant than ourselves, to stand firm in one spirit, and to strive side by side for the faith of the gospel. Jump in, and serve. Make it better. Your church isn't perfect, and if it had been, it quit being so the moment you joined it. The people in your community group have definitely sinned recently, your pastor is still wondering what in the world he got himself into, and there probably was a better way to solve that conflict, or streamline that business meeting. The people you said "good morning" to in the hallway were just bickering with their spouse on the way in, yes, the lyrics on the screen were misspelled, and finally, it is difficult to connect because both you and the people around you are shy or nervous, or hurt, or overwhelmed, or occupied, or not terribly welcoming. But to walk out on the church is to stunt your own growth, to declare that you are an island, self-sufficient, needing no one, that as it is, you've arrived well enough, and that you and Jesus have a special thing going.

Yet, by walking out, you are robbing yourself of experiencing God's love through his people and to his people. Think twice before you do it. His love will keep and sustain us, even when church is hard, all the way into the renewed creation, when all that is wrong and broken will finally be put right. And those people that you've been avoiding since that thing that happened—yeah, *that* thing—well, as a wise old pastor once counseled:

> If you account him a believer, though greatly mistaken in the subject of debate between you, the words of David to Joab, concerning Absalom, are very applicable: "Deal gently with him for my sake." The Lord loves him and bears with him; therefore you must not despise him, or treat him harshly. The Lord bears with you likewise, and expects that you should shew tenderness to others, from a sense of the much forgiveness you need yourself. In a little while you will meet in heaven; he will then be dearer to you than the nearest friend you have upon earth is to you now. Anticipate that period in your thoughts; and though you may find it necessary to oppose his errors, view him personally as a kindred soul, with whom you are to be happy in Christ forever.[5]

DISCUSSION QUESTIONS

1. Describe Jesus's relationship to the church.

2. How does our relationship with the church reflect or influence our relationship with Christ?

3. How can we deepen our relationship with God's church?

Chapter 6

HOW DO I FIND THE RIGHT CHURCH?

Mark Hallock

I know the challenges that come with trying to find a church that fits. I was born and raised in the Christian Church tradition only to become fascinated in my college years with the history, beauty and wonder of Anglicanism. My stint as an Anglican was a short one as I was soon swept away by John Calvin and a whole host of humble, godly, thoughtful Presbyterians. But then there was that infant baptism thing. This sent me down the road to where I would eventually land. You probably guessed it already. I eventually found my home as good ol' Baptist, where I now joyfully live and serve the Lord as a church member and pastor. While I praise God for all of the ways he used these different denominations and traditions to shape me and help me grow and mature as a Christ-follower, it feels so good to finally be "home."

Of course, my story is no different from so many others. This is especially true of Christians who came to faith later in life, not growing up in one particular Christian stream. In fact, as I work with college students and seminarians, this is a conversation I find myself engaged in more and more frequently.

"Where do I fit?"

"What church or denomination best aligns with my convictions?"

"How important should issues like baptism, Communion, leadership structures be in my decision?"

"How big of a deal is finding one particular church to commit to, really?"

These are important questions that thoughtful Christians must honestly ask and wrestle with. Here's what we know: **There is no perfect church.** If there were, and it was that clear, we would all be part of it! So, in light of this reality, and until we as believers are all in heaven together, how do I find a church that is a good fit for me? How do I find an (imperfect) church to give my life to? While not exhaustive, I do believe these three steps can be helpful as you seek to discern where the Lord would have you.

Step #1: Begin with hard study and humble prayer.

Prayerfully study different denominations and Christian traditions.

Learn to see the beauty of different streams. Discover what different churches and denominations believe and why. In doing this, work toward a clear understanding of where each tradition stands on both primary and secondary doctrines[1] of the Christian faith. Be sure to take the time to intentionally read and understand the best explanations and arguments from each particular denomination's best theologians throughout history. Remember to study these different traditions with a humble, teachable heart, recognizing there are very educated, godly individuals from a variety of Christian traditions who will lovingly agree to disagree on secondary matters.

Prayerfully study what you believe and why.

There two primary areas you want to think through. Where do I stand…

- **Theologically** - What are your convictions about both primary and secondary theological/doctrinal matters (beliefs)?
- **Philosophically** - What are your convictions about both primary and secondary philosophical matters (this deals with church practice and methodology…why a church does what it does in the way that it does it)?

Evaluate your options.

In light of both your theological and philosophical convictions, what churches/denominations/streams most align with your convictions? While you should never compromise your primary convictions, are there secondary convictions you are willing to agree to disagree on? What are you willing to live with…joyfully and not divisively? What are you not willing to live with? Remember, there is no perfect church this side of heaven.

Step #2: Narrow it down and make a commitment.

As you narrow it down, are there several denominations/streams that you could in good conscience be part of? Just a few? What are they? In light of this, I would encourage you to find a church within that denomination/stream that you can commit to and give your life to…not only for your sake, but for the sake of your family and other believers in the Body of Christ. In a culture where the only thing most people are committed to is being non-committal, as a Christian, this must not be your narrative. Don't jump from church to church forever. Through good and bad, go all in with an imperfect congregation and stay put. Watch what God does!

Take the time to really get to know, understand, and respect the church you are now part of. This means that while you may not agree with everything this particular church holds to or practices, this is your church now. Love it! Lean into it! Make it a huge part of your life!

"But what if I really struggle to align with a church once I've committed to it?"

If you find that you have tried but simply can't "get on board" with a church joyfully and eagerly as a result of your unshared convictions, what do you do then? If you find yourself struggling to live with, encourage, pray for, and minister alongside other believers in a congregation without becoming agitated and bitter, what then?

I think you have two main options at this point.

Option #1: Check your heart.

Check your heart and see if there is pride that you need to confess, asking the Lord, and perhaps others, to forgive you. The problem may be your own heart and an unwillingness to pursue love and unity in the way God calls us to in his Church.

Option #2: Leave well.

If you are simply unable to peacefully and joyfully live with differences you have with a church, it may be time to find a church that is a better fit for you and your family. Be sure you leave your current church well. Sadly, many people do not leave their congregation well and it causes much pain to others. As a pastor, I have been blessed by those individuals and families that have left churches I was serving well, while also experiencing many who took off without much thought to doing it the right way.

Leaving Well

Here are a five ingredients to leaving a church well:

Ingredient #1: Make sure you are leaving for the right reasons.

Search your heart, talk with your family. Are your motives and reasons for leaving solid?

Ingredient #2: Meet with your pastor.

Set up a time to talk directly to one of the pastors of your church about your leaving. You don't need to share all of your reasons or rationale, but as a matter of love and courtesy, let your pastor know you and your family have chosen to go to another church. Let your pastor know the main reasons you are leaving, but do so with humility, love and grace. Let your pastor know the things you are thankful for regarding your time at this church. Leave in a peaceful manner. This is honoring to the Lord.

Ingredient #3: Communicate clearly and lovingly with others you are close with in the church.

I recommend doing this in person, or a personal email, with individuals. Do not communicate your leaving through a mass email that could cause confusion and potential division. Satan love to divide and he works powerfully when there is confusion and lack of clarity. Communicate personally with folks.

Ingredient #4. Meet with your new pastor.

Once you find a new church, meet with your new pastor and let them know why you left your last church. Don't throw your last church under the bus. Share honestly but graciously why your family chose to leave and why you are excited about becoming part of this new church family.

Ingredient #5: Keep your former church in your prayers.

Thank God for your time at your last church and the good things he did in your life there. Continue to pray for your brothers and sisters in that congregation. This will help to fight off any bitterness that could creep into your heart toward them.

Step #3. Learn to live graciously and joyfully in your imperfect denomination/church.

Now that you have left your former congregation, there are three things to remember and implement as you transition to your new church family:

Priority #1: Distinguish between primary and secondary convictions.

Always remember there are primary and secondary convictions both philosophically and theologically. Know the difference between the two. Make sure in your heart you do not let primary matters become secondary or secondary matters become primary.

Priority #2: Learn to practice and celebrate theological hospitality.

In love, remember that even in your new church there will be differences that pop their head up once in awhile. On secondary matters, seek to journey with other believers in love and patience. Be willing and eager to learn from others, even if you disagree with them.

Priority #3: Grow in humility.

By God's grace, seek to grow in humility before the Lord, his Word, and other believers. Not one of us is inerrant in our beliefs and convictions. We all have blind spots. May we always be willing and eager to realign our beliefs and convictions as the Holy Spirit makes the teaching of Scripture clearer to us. This will involve deep humility and a willingness to "hear out" and learn from other Christians.

Christian, you were made to be part of the Body of Christ! The Lord wants to encourage you, strengthen you, transform you, and shepherd you through a local church. Don't wait! Don't remain uncommitted. Dive in and give your life to it, for your joy, the joy of others, and the glory of God!

DISCUSSION QUESTIONS

1. What is your theological journey that has led you to the church or denomination that you are in today?

2. Brainstorm some of the benefits of being committed to one church for the long haul.

3. Where are you at with your current church involvement? What's your next step to be more involved (i.e. join a Bible study, start serving)?

Chapter 7

WHY DO WE CELEBRATE THE LORD'S SUPPER EVERY WEEK?

Nathan Piotrowski

> If a man be hungry and you bring him flowers or pictures, they do not satisfy, but bread does fully satisfy. So Jesus Christ, the bread of the soul, satisfies; He satisfied the eye with beauty, the heart with sweetness, the conscience with peace.
>
> – Thomas Watson[1]

Throughout the world, each week as churches gather for worship, they celebrate the Lord's supper. It is a sweet time of joyful remembrance which we believe is important enough to make our regular practice. What makes it such an integral part of the life of our churches? There are at least three reasons. First, Communion is a proclamation of the gospel, the essential message of Christianity. Second, a regular celebration of Communion is commanded by Scripture and was practiced frequently by the early Church. And third, remembering Christ in Communion is deeply encouraging for every believer in their relationship with Jesus Christ.

Communion as Gospel Proclamation

The most critical and essential focus of the entire Bible is the gospel. Simply put, the gospel is the life-giving news of who Christ is and what he has done in redeeming sinners. This special emphasis is revealed throughout Scripture. Jesus even explicitly taught his disciples that the entire Old Testament was written about himself and what he would do.

> "These are my words that I spoke to you while I was still with you, that everything written about me in the Law of Moses and the Prophets and the Psalms must be fulfilled." Then he opened their minds to understand the Scriptures, and said to them, "Thus it is written, that the Christ should suffer and on the third day rise from the dead, and that repentance for the forgiveness of sins should be proclaimed in his name to all nations, beginning from Jerusalem" (Luke 24:44b-47).

Paul emphasizes the same gospel message in 1 Corinthians,

> For I delivered to you as of *first importance* what I also received: that Christ died for our sins in accordance with the Scriptures, that he was buried, that he was raised on the third day in accordance with the Scriptures (1 Corinthians 15:3-4)[emphasis mine].

Further, in the two preceding verses, Paul says that they have already heard and received this message, but that it is necessary for them to be reminded of it again.

> Now I would remind you, brothers, of the gospel I preached to you, which you received, in which you stand, and by which you are being saved, if you hold fast to the word I preached to you—unless you believed in vain (1 Corinthians 15:1-2).

The Corinthians needed to hold onto the gospel or they would have "believed in vain."

The same is still true for every Christian today. We must continue to hear and hold fast to what Christ has done. To assume the gospel is to begin to lose the gospel. Therefore, this essential message of the cross must be proclaimed continually.

We are familiar with the gospel being proclaimed in a sermon. In addition to this, we have an incredibly profound picture and practice by which we are commanded to proclaim the gospel. This is the celebration of the Lord's Supper, or Communion. Paul writes, "For as often as you eat this bread and drink the cup, *you proclaim the Lord's death until he comes*" (1 Corinthians 11:26) [emphasis added]. Celebrating Communion in our churches together is a declaration of what Christ has done. When the bread is broken, it is both a picture and a proclamation of Christ's body, broken on the cross. When the cup is held up, it is both a picture and a proclamation that Christ's blood was spilled on the cross. And, when Christians eat the bread and drink the cup, it is an amazing picture and proclamation that Christ is ours and we are his, by faith, through his sacrifice for us. As a necessary reminder of the cross, Communion also compels us to continue to share the Good News of Jesus "until he comes." As the bride of Christ, believers eagerly anticipate the bridegroom's return. Furthermore, when we partake in the Lord's Supper as a church body, we experience unity as together we proclaim both his death and his imminent return. Communion is a bonding experience for the family of God.

This is also why the Lord's Supper is exclusive; it's for believers only. Communion is not a means of grace, and it has no significance for those outside of Christ. However, we encourage those who have not yet come to Christ by faith to use this time to reflect on their state before him. At our church, we post two prayers on the screen during Communion: one is intended to stimulate further reflection and introspection for believers, and the other is for those who lack faith in Christ and may be seeking him. When unbelievers remain in their seats and don't partake in the meal intended only for followers of Christ, it can be a poignant time of asking themselves what is holding them back from receiving the salvation freely offered in Christ.

Therefore, in the regular practice of Communion, we have an incredible safeguard against neglecting the message of the cross for both believers and unbelievers. Reclaiming the centrality of the cross in our churches today is a much-needed corrective. And, celebrating Communion each week does just that. It protects the priority of the gospel in our churches and even in our own hearts.

Communion as Command and Practice

God's Word has much to say about celebrating Communion. Although weekly Communion is never *explicitly* prescribed, it was a regular practice of the early Church in keeping with Jesus' teaching. In fact, the Scriptures seem to indicate the Lord's Supper was celebrated *every* time Christians gathered for worship.

Jesus instituted the Lord's Supper on the night he was betrayed (Matthew 26:26-28; Mark 14:22-24; Luke 22:19-20). It is then immediately picked up by the early Church in Acts 2:42, "And they devoted themselves to the apostles' teaching and the fellowship, to the breaking of bread and the prayers." Breaking of bread is again mentioned in verse 46. One commentary defines it this way:

> The 'breaking of bread' is best understood as a reference to the ordinary meals that the believers regularly shared, during which they remembered Jesus' death on the cross for the forgiveness of sins and for the establishment of the new covenant, linked with the command to remember Jesus and his sacrifice during meals.[2]

Years later, after the gospel had spread across the Roman Empire through church planting, the Apostle Paul landed in Troas on his third missionary journey. In Acts chapter 20 verse 7, we see the first reference to a weekly worship gathering. "On the first day of the week, when we were gathered together to break bread, Paul talked with them, intending to depart on the next day, and he prolonged his speech until midnight." Remarkably, the text indicates the purpose of this regular gathering was to *break bread*. In other words, celebrating Communion was such an essential part of what happened when Christians gathered that the term "breaking of bread" is practically used as a euphemism for the gathering! Luke, the author of Acts, further assumes his readers would be so familiar with this practice that it did not even require an explanation.

A final key text to understanding the importance of the Lord's Supper in the early Church is found in 1 Corinthians 11:17-26. In short, Scripture tells us the church in Corinth was having problems in how they were celebrating Communion. In the text, it is clear this was a regular practice whenever they gathered. However, Paul writes that there were divisions in the church and certain factions weren't waiting for others to arrive. Some were gorging themselves while others were going hungry. Paul rebukes them by saying, "When you come together, it is not the Lord's Supper that you eat" (1 Corinthians 11:20). The phrase "when you come together" refers to the regular gathering of the believers for worship. Part of that was a meal, which they intended to be the Lord's Supper. But Paul is saying, "No way! You are not practicing this celebration in a manner which is pleasing to the Lord." Another instructive phrase in verse 25 is "as often as you drink." This, again, indicates it was a regular practice when they were coming together.

Based on these texts, it seems clear that celebrating Communion was the consistent practice of the early Christians. When they gathered together weekly for worship, they were celebrating Communion.

Communion as Intimacy with Christ

One of the main objections against celebrating Communion every week is that such frequency could cause the practice to lose its meaning. Although this is a real danger, this argument fails to consider one of the main purposes—indeed, blessings—of Communion. Looking to Christ during this special time of remembrance is a precious opportunity for a Christian to experience powerful reassurance and intimacy with Christ.

A Christian is one who has seen the depth of his or her sin and who has answered the call of Jesus to come—to be forgiven and made clean, to be rescued and made righteous, to be accepted into God's family by his sheer grace, to be made new and resurrected to new life—through faith in Christ alone. So, for Christians, Communion is a *sweet* time! Through Communion, we are reminded again of the One who loved us and gave himself for us. Jesus Christ is our provision; he is our life. Every time we gather and celebrate this meal, our gaze is once again fixed on our Savior and what he has done for us. He is the One who, through his cruel death on a cross, absorbed in his perfect body the wrath of God we deserve. In the powerful practice of Communion, we are reminded that his body was broken for us. His blood was spilled for us. And by eating, we proclaim that he is ours, because he has made us his. In short, to celebrate Communion is to commune with the One we love.

Indeed, remembering our Lord and Savior on the cross holds special significance and encouragement for every believer. For those of us who are weighed down in sin and guilt and shame, Communion is a response of faith. We come, once again, to the One who has washed us clean, the One who has empowered us to walk in newness of life (Romans 8:1).

For those of us who have grown numb to sin, callous and indifferent, we are confronted with the awful seriousness of our sin.

His punishment fits our crime. We are called to come, once again, in fresh repentance to the One who bought us and adopted us that we might be holy and blameless before him (Ephesians 1:4-5; Romans 6:12-14, 22).

For those of us who are gripped by sadness or loss, for those who are lonely, we draw near to the One who came near to us. We taste and see the One who loved us first and who loved us to the very end. He is the One who knows our suffering because he has suffered and because he suffers with us (Matthew 1:23; Hebrews 2:14-18).

For those of us who are slipping into a pattern of trying to please God through our own merit, we are called to come. And we come empty-handed—not in our own strength, or with our promised good intentions, or with a record of what we have done for God. We remember that he is the One who has *finished* the work. We come and rest (John 19:30; Matthew 11:28-30).

For those of us who are in a season of joy, and even trial, we come to the One who is the source of our joy and who himself is our greatest joy (Psalm 16:11). We are "looking to Jesus, the founder and perfecter of our faith, who for the joy that was set before him endured the cross, despising the shame, and is seated at the right hand of the throne of God" (Hebrews 12:2).

Far from some austere and ritualistic emphasis, God's Word calls all people to come and experience true intimacy with the triune God. David exhorted, "Oh, taste and see that the LORD is good! Blessed is the man who takes refuge in him!" (Psalm 34:8). To the woman at the well, we hear Jesus say,

> Everyone who drinks of this water will be thirsty again, but whoever drinks of the water that I will give him will never be thirsty again. The water that I will give him will become in him a spring of water welling up to eternal life (John 4:13-14).

For Christians celebrating Communion, the mystery of Jesus' words are revealed to our hearts:

> Whoever feeds on my flesh and drinks my blood has eternal life, and I will raise him up on the last day. For my flesh is true food, and my blood is true drink. Whoever feeds on my flesh and drinks my blood abides in me, and I in him (John 6:54-56).

This is nothing less than our experience of spiritual and eternal life which flows from the fact that Jesus Christ is intimately with us, even *in* us, by his Spirit.

Throughout Scripture we are called to experience Christ, who is deeply refreshing and satisfying. And, one day, our faith will become sight as we see him face to face! David's prayer will be answered, "One thing have I asked of the Lord, that will I seek after: that I may dwell in the house of the Lord, all the days of my life, to gaze upon the beauty of the Lord, and to inquire in his temple" (Psalm 27:4). Communion is a taste of this glorious hope. Why would we not want to remember this each week?

The gospel, the priority of Scripture, is clearly proclaimed in Communion. Jesus commanded his followers to practice it, and the early Church obeyed that command. And Communion is a deeply satisfying and intimate experience for those who love Jesus. For these reasons, we are passionately committed to celebrating Jesus Christ together each week through Communion.

DISCUSSION QUESTIONS

1. How does taking Communion weekly proclaim the gospel?

2. What season of life are you in and how does God minister to you through Communion in this season?

3. How can you deepen your intimacy with Jesus through Communion?

Chapter 8

HOW DO I ENGAGE PRACTICALLY IN THE MISSION OF GOD?

Seth Van Essen

We live in an age dominated by professionals: professionals in sports, finance, home repair, medicine, fitness, auto repair, and the restaurant business. While we are grateful for professionals in many areas of our lives, it can shift our perspective when it comes to faith and spirituality. We have our pastors, priests, and clergy that can act and operate as professionals; they are the ones we call to pray for us, give us advice, spiritually feed us, console us, officiate our weddings, and someday our funerals. The gift and role of a pastor is priceless and God-given. In fact, it is biblical and essential to the health of any local church. However, we often have replicated the world's model of experts in Christianity and have formed categories such as "super Christians" or "professional Christian." This is not the design God has invited us into or intended.

In order to answer the question of how we engage practically in the mission of God, we must first understand how God designed his mission. God's intention for Christ followers is that all who believe in Jesus are called priests; theologians call this the "priesthood of all believers." This concept means that all believers have direct access to God and a purpose in the grand story of the gospel. Before Jesus came to earth, God required a priest to be the mediator between his people and himself. As mediators, the priests were set apart, lived differently, engaged God's people, and spoke to them about the things of God. These priests served a unique purpose in God's grander story of redemption. However, with Christ everything changed!

Jesus is our perfect and eternal high priest. After Christ we no longer need priests to act for us or represent us to God. The apostle Peter says, "You yourselves like living stones are being built up as a spiritual house, to be a holy priesthood, to offer spiritual sacrifices acceptable to God through Jesus Christ" (1 Peter 2:5). He goes on to say "But you are a chosen generation, a royal priesthood, a holy nation, his own special people, that you may proclaim the praises of him who called you out of darkness into his marvelous light..." (1 Peter 2:9). Likewise, the author of Hebrews makes it clear we can approach God directly with confidence because Jesus is our high priest and mediator (Hebrews 4:14-16). Therefore, if you are in Christ, you are a priest. You are also a witness (Acts 1:8), an ambassador (2 Corinthians 5:20), and one who testifies (Acts 10:42, Acts 20:21, Acts 20:24) to Good News. Scripture claims these powerful words and identities to be true of those who are now followers of Jesus.

The Bible never calls us gurus, professionals, or masters of the things of Jesus. This should be hopeful for us! No matter how long you have known Jesus, no matter what you know or do not know, you are invited to give witness to what Jesus has done and is doing in you. You are invited into his story.

Many enter into participation in God's mission as a way to give back to God, as a means to find justification or earn forgiveness. To be clear, we are saved by grace and grace alone: no works, no words, no boldness, no kindness, no morals, no actions, no service, no attitude, nor church attendance can add to what Jesus has done. Until we first personally know and have experienced the love, acceptance, kindness, grace, and healing from Jesus, we have nothing to offer others. It is out of the overflow of what we have received from Christ, that we can testify, witness, and represent Christ to other people. Only then can we participate rightly!

One of the best invitations to participation in his kingdom work is the Great Commission in Matthew 28:16-19. Jesus says,

> All authority in heaven and on earth has been given to me. Go therefore, and make disciples of all nations, baptizing them in the name of the Father and of the Son and of the Holy Spirit, teaching them to observe all that I have commanded you. And behold, I am with you always, to the end of the age.

We often think that this command is for the exceptional Christians who "know" all the things Jesus taught. However, one of the most hopeful verses that often gets overlooked in talking about this passage is in verse 17. This verse starts with an honest assessment of his disciples, a bunch of average nobodies, which stood beside Jesus. They were all followers that deserted him weeks before. Verse 17 reads, "And when they saw him they worshiped him, but some doubted." What! Did I read that right? Some doubted? They saw Jesus die and now there, right in front of them, Jesus stood alive, and yet still some doubted! And more than this, before Jesus invites his followers into one of the greatest journeys, the Bible clarifies that it is for all of us. This journey, to follow him, is even for the doubters. That includes those of us who do not have it all figured out, who have not "arrived", and those still trying to make sense of it all. "Go," Jesus said and tell them what you have seen, what I have done, and what I have said. This is so encouraging!

Another powerful and necessary truth to understand is: we who follow Jesus have the power inside of us to actually put our hands to doing and accomplishing what he calls us to do. This is not willpower or your own self-motivation, skill, or desire. Not at all! If we are in Christ, we have the same Holy Spirit in us that raised Christ from the dead and he is at work inside of us to also continually raise us up to new life. (Romans 8:9-11). This is the Holy Spirit that Jesus said was a better gift than having Jesus himself still physically walking with us. (John 16: 7-10). The Holy Spirit is the one that will give us words when we need them (Luke 21:15), will give us the characteristics or "fruit" of Christ (Galatians 5:22-25), will protect and safeguard our faith (Ephesian 4:30), comfort us in our time of need (1 Corinthians 1:3-5), and remind us of all the things he taught (John 14:26), and more.

By deepening our understanding of these foundational truths, we can have a fuller and more clear perspective to enter the conversation of practical ways to engage God's Kingdom in our lives.

Listed below are some ideas, thoughts, and creative ways to think about how the gospel applies practically to all areas in our lives. This list is not an all-inclusive list but is intended to encourage creative thinking and new ways to see the gospel at work. As we are more aware & looking, we begin to see more of the ways that God is at work in the world and we can join him.

10 Practical Ideas for Everyone to Seek God's Kingdom Every Day.

Idea #1: Just do something.

I was once told that it is easier to steer a moving car than one that is sitting still. God uses our experiences, choices, and activities to shape us, move us, and change us. Often, our fear can cripple us from doing anything, and sometimes we spend our whole life trying to learn about the things of Jesus and never just put into practice what we already know. You might be surprised how much you actually know about what Jesus taught. Now put it into practice and just do something!

Idea #2: Overlap your life with those far from Jesus.

Intentionally choose to make the routines of your life engage, overlap, encounter, and rub shoulders with those at different places in their journey with God. In our lives, we all have people at different places along their journey but often we do not engage them intentionally. Some examples of intentionally engaging others include: learning your bank teller's/grocer's/barista's/postman's name, asking them hobbies they enjoy, asking them what is currently bringing them joy, fear, or anxiety. Maybe ask them about their kids or closest relationship in life. Pray for them. Meet your kids' friends' parents, invite a co-worker to lunch, take a walk around the block and talk to whomever you meet, get on a local sports team, invite friends, neighbors, co-workers over to do what you normally do (watch sports, play video games, garden, play music…whatever!).

Idea #3: Become a beggar.

Jim Misloski, a former elder at Calvary Church Englewood, encouraged me to become a beggar. He told me of a time when he was digging something up in his yard, and rather than grabbing his own shovel from his garage, he became the beggar and went to ask his neighbor to borrow a shovel. Choose to need a cup of sugar, an egg, a rake, or a helping hand. People like to help and to be a part of something, to contribute and be needed. Becoming the beggar provides a great opportunity to overlap life and engage our neighbors. We follow Jesus as he does this with the Samaritan woman by vulnerably asking her, "will you give me a drink?" (John

4:7). The Samaritan woman's life was changed that day! Become a beggar.

Idea #4: Start a 2% Fund.

Intentionally choose to set aside 2% of your income each month to spend on others. Often, we can get lazy and let the church do all of the work of leveraging our money for the work of the gospel, instead of seeking ways to give to God's kingdom work in additional ways as well. While the church genuinely seeks to be good stewards of our money and needs our tithes and offerings to be able to function for the work of ministry, we know that God wants our hearts to be sensitive and engaged to the movements of the Spirit. The 2% fund is a great way to intentionally be on your knees in prayer, asking the Holy Spirit to keep your heart in-tune to the needs around you. Be free with this! This can be money that is used to encourage other believers or engage those who don't know Jesus. Some examples include: inviting a neighbor to dinner and paying for it, buying and cooking fancy steak and drinks for someone to show how the gospel is lavish and abundant even when undeserved, taking the single mom and her kids to a baseball game, buying the groceries of the person behind you in line, taking time to invite the homeless man to eat lunch, buying gift cards and finding strangers to bless, or giving a gift to a missionary, pastor, or someone in the ministry.

Idea #5: Value the power of proximity.

Michelle Ferrigno Warren, a co-founder of a local Denver inner city ministry named Open Door Ministries, says in her book *The Power of Proximity*,

> Being proximate is necessary to engage brokenness because it transforms our lens. We cannot learn from a distance. We need deeper, more

informed perspective into ourselves, our communities, and the restoration we all seek.[1]

As Christians we need to be present and near to the poor, hurting, broken, downtrodden, and outcast. This takes reorienting life, sharing life, and inviting people into our lives. This can feel scary. It can be exposing. How can we reorient our lives to be proximate to those not like ourselves?

Idea #6: Step into someone's problem.

Sound like a dumb idea? Jesus did it. Jesus spent time with lepers, who were social outcasts. Not only were they outcasts, but they were literally considered to be untouchables. They were kicked out of family, could not get jobs, and had to beg for food. Talk about problems! Jesus not only joined them and spent time with them, but he also gave them dignity. We know by the accounts in the gospels that Jesus healed some lepers, but he did not heal all of them. Sometimes in our world, entering into someone's problem simply to be with them is one of the best ministry opportunities we can have. Not fixing their problem, not changing it, not bringing our knowledge or answers or solutions, but just being with someone in their problem shows compassion, care, and the love of Christ. Being together and with people in the mess or problem, grows our faith, trust, and hope in Jesus. When there is nothing else to rely on, we get to wait on Jesus. Is this not the way of the Kingdom? Jesus speaks to this saying, "blessed are the poor in spirit, blessed are the merciful, blessed are the meek, blessed are those who hunger and thirst for righteousness" (Matthew 5 & 6).

Idea #7: Don't forget the basics.

Be kind, ask questions, smile, serve. Author and Speaker, Carl Medearis says some profound thoughts about this in his book, *42 Seconds*.

> We forget that kindness is a fruit of the Spirit...It's one of the top qualities we're to exhibit if we have the Spirit of Jesus in our lives. So that's why, if we're going to be like Jesus in our everyday interactions, we have to go back to the basics. Kindness 101. Encouragement to be nice to those around us. Basic human being sort of stuff. These are the things we sometimes miss in the busyness and craziness of life...It's basically impossible to introduce our neighbors and coworkers to Jesus if we're not kind to them.[2]

These practical and basic rhythms of kindness in our lives are vital to engaging those who need Jesus.

Idea #8: Be A Good Neighbor.

In the book *The Art of Neighboring* by Jay Pathak and David Runyon, they give one of the simplest challenges to being a good neighbor: to learn the names of the immediate neighbors around you.[3] A name is personal and starts a connection. A name opens the door to friendship. It gives a personal connection to begin a conversation and relationship. Treat your neighbor like you want to be treated. Start by knowing their name.

Idea #9: Serve your local church.

Churches are built upon volunteers giving time to serve in different areas: from greeting, community groups, bible studies, outreach events, to name a few. The church needs people. It is not a building but a body of believers and as such, needs people participating in this living body. The church is a safe and welcoming place to practice your gifting and stretch yourself to try new things.

Idea #10: Do something impossible.

Our culture often misquotes 1 Corinthians 10:13 when they say God will not stretch us beyond what we can handle. They apply this verse to all situations in life, rather than specifically to temptation as the Scripture quotes. This is where we go awry. Throughout the Bible we see followers of God who are given or are asked to do far more than they can do themselves. Abraham, Moses, Esther, David, Paul, and the list could go on. This is also true for us who follow Jesus today. Our confidence is in the fact that he calls himself faithful to his people, to us.

Rely on the one who is faithful and step into the things of his Kingdom. I challenge you to begin to seek the Lord in prayer, asking for impossible things that are aligned to his Kingdom, and see what God calls you into. Some examples of this could be fostering, adopting, starting a new career, buying a house to use for ministry, actively engaging in the reconciliation of a broken relationship, championing change for a local or national law, choosing to fight for freedom from addiction or other sin. Dream big, ask big!

My prayer is that you find hope, encouragement, and empowerment as a Christ follower. You are invited to participate as a witness in his grand story! Be creative, be engaged, be intentional, and do all of these things in community.

DISCUSSION QUESTIONS

1. How does Jesus equip us to engage in His work in the world?

2. How has God wired you uniquely to serve your church and your community?

3. What is one practical thing that you can do today to start living out these ten suggestions?

Chapter 9

WHAT IS MY ROLE IN GLOBAL MISSIONS?

Kevin Hasenack

> Every Christian here is either a missionary or an imposter.[1]
> - C.H. Spurgeon

I'd like to make something very clear right from the beginning. Whether you've been a Christian for a few hours, or Christian for most of your life, you have been given a task. A great task to tell others about Jesus. That means in your own home, in your neighborhood, and to the ends of the earth. You have been asked by God to make Jesus known in the world around you.

You might have some questions on how to share your faith. This chapter won't fully jump into the nuts and bolts of 'how-to', but rather talk about the specific questions of: "Do we need global missions? and What's my role in telling other cultures about Jesus?"

I may have already lost you. I understand that this may not be something you have thought about much before. Some of you may be saying, "I'm not a missionary," or "why tell people of a different culture about Jesus? Aren't there plenty of people that are just like me to whom I can better share the gospel with in my context?" These are normal thoughts to wrestle with as we continue our discussion.

I think it's best to clearly state that solely focusing on cross culture ministry (gospel work amongst a people of a different culture context than your own) may not be the way that the Lord has called you. What I am saying is that cross-culture ministry is tragically neglected by many churches and believers. It is not the job of missions organizations to reach those different than us. It's not a job for "someone else." This is a task for every church, and ultimately every believer to tell all people about Jesus.

> Specifically, it's the primary responsibility of every pastor of every local church to love people in that church and to love people in that community, all toward the ultimate end that the name of Christ might be praised among every group of people on the planet. That's what the Spirit of Christ wants, so that's what every Christian, every pastor, and every local church should want.[2]

Where does this leave us? Should we all immediately put down this book, jump on a plane to some far-away place and upon landing on the ground there burn our passport? Not exactly. John Piper put it so well when he said, "Missions is not the ultimate goal of the church. Worship is. Missions exists because worship doesn't. Worship is ultimate, not missions, because God is ultimate not man."[3]

Too often we focus on a task that is off course. We lose sight of the ultimate purpose—the glory of God. John Stott said,

> Here lies the supreme missionary motivation. It is neither obedience to the Great Commission, nor compassion for the lost, nor excitement over the gospel, but zeal (even jealousy) for the honor of Christ's name...no incentive is stronger than the longing that Christ should be given the honor that is due His name.[4]

God's Heart for the Nations

If we are to better understand the answer to the main question, we have to take a closer look at a key principle that all Christians should grasp. You and I, as believers, should be about what God is about. We should love the things that our Heavenly Father loves. One of those things is God's love for the world.

God has a heart for the nations. He loves all people, all tribes, all languages. We see this picture from the book of Revelation.

After this I looked, and behold, a great multitude that no one could number, from every nation, from all tribes and peoples and languages, standing before the throne and before the Lamb, clothed in white robes, with palm branches in their hands, and crying out with a loud voice, "Salvation belongs to our God who sits on the throne, and to the Lamb!" (Revelation 7:9-10).

This is not just the picture we see at the end, but a theme we see though out the entirety of the Bible. From Genesis to Revelation, we can see a glorious thread showing us his heart for all people, and by the power of the Holy Spirit, what posture our hearts should have toward them as well.

How to Grow Your Heart for the Nations

1. The Holy Spirit will guide you in spirit and in truth.

> When the Spirit of truth comes, he will guide you into all the truth, for he will not speak on his own authority, but whatever he hears he will speak, and he will declare to you the things that are to come (John 16:13).

Every time that we come into contact with the Word of God (reading, hearing, memorizing), you should be faithfully interacting with the Holy Spirit. Listen to what is being said to you, and allow the Spirit to guide you in your next steps.

> In a culture of evangelism, people who love Jesus work together as instruments in the grand symphony of God's work. We don't always know what the next piece will be—the Holy Spirit orchestrates that. But if we are focused on Him and is direction, we get to be a part of his work in people's lives.[5]

2. The Word of God is living, powerful, and transforming.

If you are like me, often I rush though my time with the Lord. I have my mind elsewhere, and many mornings I'm full of selfishness, looking for what I can get out of my time with him. I have to remind myself that God's Word is powerful, living and transforming.

> For the word of God is living and active, sharper than any two-edged sword, piercing to the division of soul and of spirit, of joints and of marrow, and discerning the thoughts and intentions of the heart (Hebrews 4:12).

Don't rush though your study. Take your time. Our interaction with God's Word should always challenge us, push us toward action, and change us to become more like his son, Jesus. We live in a time where we seem to have less and less time, but that time is there if you are willing to intentionally make your time with the Lord happen.

3. Memorizing and meditation will help you move from reading and interpreting the Bible though your own biases and filter.

If you are anything like me, your head might be full of lots of useless facts. There is a lot of sports trivia, song lyrics, and random facts that might help me win Jeopardy. Sadly, there isn't as much Scripture as I want there to be stuck in my brain. Yet I have found over the years that memorizing and meditating on Scripture helps me see the world much closer to the way that God does. This is especially true for aligning my heart closer to His.

Jeff Lewis tells us, "Meditation may seem mystical, but it is an essential element to gain understanding beyond the surface meaning and application of a passage."[6] How true is that!?! When we take time to meditate on the passage we have just heard or read, often times the Lord will show us something we have not seen after being with that passage many times in the past.

The book of Psalms has so many verses that tell us the importance of meditation: "But his delight is in the law of the Lord, and on his law he meditates day and night" (Psalm 1:2). Or this one from Psalm 119:97,99: "Oh, how I love your law! I meditate on it all day long. I have more insight that all my teachers, for I meditate on your statutes." You will not discover all that God wants to teach you if you ignore this important discipline. Learn to bring this discipline into your daily life. Even as you fall asleep, meditate on his word: "...I think of you thought the watches of the night" (Psalm 63:6).

Closing Thoughts

Whatever your job may be, know that the nations are at your doorstep. It has never been easier to engage in cross cultural ministry and introduce them to the gospel. Every person on earth needs to hear the gospel. "The human mind is the same everywhere. Its sins may take another form, but there are just the same difficulties in one place as in another."[7]

I pray that God gives you the boldness to tell others about him. I pray that you begin to follow after his heart for the nations. I pray that we begin to not only see Jesus become non-ignorable close to home, but to the ends of the Earth. I pray that you would be still before him, listen to his voice, and know that he will be exulted in all the Earth (Psalm 46:10).

> ### DISCUSSION QUESTIONS:
>
> 1. Do you have a heart for the nations? What's keeping you from that?
>
> 2. How will you engage in telling others about Jesus?
>
> 3. What are 2 different ways you can pray for Jesus to be known in the ends of the Earth?
>
> 4. How else can you support God's work around the world?

Chapter 10

WHAT DOES THE BIBLE HAVE TO SAY ABOUT SOCIAL JUSTICE?

Spencer Parish

> God loves and defends those with the least economic and social power, and so should we. That is what it means to 'do justice.'[1]
> – Timothy Keller

Information Overload

We are the most well-informed society the world has ever known. We are bombarded with more messages through more mediums than ever before. This abundance of information has both benefits and challenges. One of the benefits of living in this era is that virtually no societal ill goes unnoticed in our day. Issues such as abortion, sex trafficking, working-class poverty, prison reform, and many others continue to gain greater attention from our collective conscience, which is the first step toward alleviating the suffering of those involved - awareness. However, it can be overwhelming trying to discern which of these issues we're called to engage in, not to mention the question of what that engagement should look like. So what exactly does the Christian faith have to say about issues like these? How should we, as Christians, think and act with regard to them? What follows is a very brief attempt to answer these questions.

A Rich Heritage

We would do well to begin by observing that Bible-believing, Jesus-loving Christians have been on the front lines in the fight against injustice since the time of Christ. Clear back in the second and third centuries, the ancient world experienced great plagues, which some historians claim may have killed from a quarter to a third of the population. The only people caring for the ill and providing the dignity of burial to the deceased? Christians. Rather than fleeing, they stayed with the sick and dying and cared for them, risking their own health in the process.[2]

The fight to end the African slave trade and institutional slavery in 19th century England was led by Christians, as well, most notably William Wilberforce, a member of the "Clapham Sect", a group of Christians committed to fighting injustice in their time. Wilberforce petitioned Parliament for decades before seeing slavery abolished three days before his death in 1833.[3] These serve as a small sample of the many ways Christians have pursued justice throughout the centuries. So what drove these Christians to serve and minister to the sick and the oppressed? What does the Scripture have to say about these kinds of issues?

Imago Dei

Foundational to the Christian concern for the welfare of all people is the *imago dei* - the image of God. This basic tenet of our faith is clearly expounded all the way back in the beginning, in Genesis 1:27:

> So God created man in his own image,

in the image of God he created him;
male and female he created them.

A commitment to this belief, that every human to ever live has been made in God's image, should naturally lead to joyfully, passionate service of our fellow man, and has done so among Christians for centuries, even millenia. This is due to the fact that the *imago dei* carries with it significant implications. If all people are made in the image of God, this implies that all people are valuable, and worthy of love, respect, and dignity. No other worldview provides such a firm foundation for charity as the biblical worldview, because the Christian faith alone instructs us of the *imago dei*.

A Special Concern

However, the roots of our involvement in social justice run even deeper. It is not only the *imago dei* that fuels our efforts, but God's special concern for the afflicted, the oppressed, the poor, and the marginalized. Scripture is replete with evidence that God is especially concerned with those whom the world neglects. It is also filled with commands to be like God and care for these people. Take James 2:15-17, for example:

> If a brother or sister is without clothing and in need of daily food, and one of you says to them, "Go in peace, be warmed and be filled," and yet you do not give them what is necessary for their body, what use is that? Even so faith, if it has no works, is dead, being by itself.

There can be little dispute that Christians are indeed called to fight against injustice in the world. To care for victims of sex trafficking. To empower ex-convicts to get their lives on track. To come alongside and care for widows. To take in and love orphans. To serve as foster parents. Christians ought to be the most zealous and passionate about these causes. About this, there is no doubt.

And yet…

Heart Matters

And yet, if we are to truly honor the Lord with our lives, it is not enough to fight the right battles. We must fight for the right reasons. God is not simply after transformed behavior in his people but transformed hearts.

Some engage in these causes motivated by guilt. Guilt that their life is so easy compared to the single mother's, for example. And without realizing it, they begin serving (a right action) to alleviate their own sense of guilt (a selfish motive). One of the dangers we face is placing a burden upon one another (or ourselves) to pursue justice for all, resulting in guilt and shame. Therefore, we must be careful, "not turn every possibility into a responsibility and every opportunity into an ought."[4]

So, what is the right motive for "doing justice" in the world? Why is it Christians have been about social justice throughout history? The answer lies in the gospel.

The Right Motive

Tim Keller writes, "The Bible gives believers two basic motivations – joyful awe before the goodness of God's creation, and the experience of God's grace in redemption."[5] What is it that ought to drive us to care about injustice? The realization that God cared about us when no one else did. An awareness that we are "poor in spirit" (Matthew 5:3). An understanding that when we had nothing of spiritual value to offer to God, he came to us. He was generous toward us, giving us the grace we needed, but didn't deserve. In fact, when we were so far in spiritual debt that we had absolutely no hope of ever making it into the black, he paid the ultimate price to set us free. Christ died to pay our ransom. Despite the fact that our spiritual poverty was our own fault, he did not withhold his mercy, but showed compassion upon the most needy – us.

When we realize that, how can we possibly look upon the poor and needy with anything but compassion? It is the experience of God's grace in the gospel that should motivate us to be compassionate toward the lowest in society's eyes. Christians ought to be passionately and joyfully engaged in fighting against injustice in the world, seeking the welfare of all people, as a response to God's gracious and merciful action toward us.

The Right Mission

But we would be remiss in this discussion if we did not address a common error in our day with regard to social justice, and that is the mistake of making this into the primary mission of God and his people. Even while we ought to passionately pursue the good of all people, we must keep in view the ultimate good – to be made right with God. To find forgiveness of sin, adoption into God's family, and eternal life in Christ. To enter into God's Kingdom forever – not merely to taste it now.

If we eliminate world poverty, outlaw abortion, eradicate racism, and achieve world peace, but fail to preach the gospel to those who are far from God, we have missed the point. We have given the world what they want, but not what they most desperately need.

The Purpose for Which God Created the World

Even as we engage in the fight against injustice, we must remember that at the end of the day, this world is not our home. Our ultimate hope lies not in this life, but the next. Our great, glorious gospel does not promise ease in this life, but infinite joy and peace when this life ends. The gospel promises that through repentance and faith in Christ we receive the forgiveness of our sins, and are imputed with Christ's righteousness so that when we stand before God someday (as we all will), we will not be told "I never knew you, depart from me" (Matthew 7:23b) but will instead be welcomed with open arms, like the prodigal son in Luke 15.

God's ultimate goal is to create a new heavens and a new earth where he will reign in perfect justice, and he will be glorified forever, as all the redeemed, washed by Christ's blood, rejoice in his grace, mercy, beauty, and manifold perfection. This is where all of cosmic history is heading. And God does not desire "that any should perish, but that all should come to repentance" (2 Peter 3:9). God has not promised to change our circumstances in this life, but that in Christ, we can endure any and all circumstances, knowing that,

> he has caused us to be born again to a living hope through the resurrection of Jesus Christ from the dead, to an inheritance that is imperishable, undefiled, and unfading, kept in heaven for you, who by God's power are being guarded through faith for a salvation ready to be revealed in the last time. (1 Peter 1:3-5)

Our primary calling as disciples of Jesus is not to bring about God's Kingdom through our efforts. It is to lead others to the well of eternal life, Jesus himself, so that they will live forever with us in the Kingdom he will consummate at his return. To help them find this glorious, imperishable, undefiled, unfading inheritance! To help them find salvation!

Our efforts to bring about justice in the world today ought to serve to advance this mission. This doesn't mean we only serve people we think might come to faith - we serve anyone and everyone. It simply means that we serve them with a dual hope - that their suffering here and now might be alleviated, and that their eternal suffering might be avoided! We serve them with the hope that they will come to faith, knowing that whatever results our efforts may accomplish here are only temporary. Any justice or peace we're able to help bring to people today may be gone tomorrow - taken away by the world, or by death.

There will be a day when justice rules, and evil and wickedness and oppression will cease. But that will only happen when Christ brings about the new heavens and the new earth. Let us remember that, even as we seek to bring about peace and justice here and now.

DISCUSSION QUESTIONS

1. How does the *imago Dei* impact our view of the people around us?

2. As we fight injustice, how can we strive to keep our motives pure?

3. What does the author say our dual hope is as we serve people?

part three

HONEST QUESTIONS ABOUT...

THE GOD-CENTERED LIFE

Chapter 11

IF I GAVE MY LIFE TO JESUS, WHY IS MY LIFE SO HARD?

Dan Freng

> In the world, you will have tribulation. But take heart; I have overcome the world.
> – Jesus (John 16:33)

When I became a Christian in the summer of 1998, two things happened in my life simultaneously: my life was significantly better and my life was suddenly harder. My life was significantly better because Jesus had saved me. He had forgiven me of my sins and had rescued me from God's wrath. The burden of my guilt had been lifted. I was alive to joy and peace and hope in a way that I had never been before. Jesus was so real to me and I experienced a friendship with him through his word and prayer that was unlike anything I had ever known. My life was significantly better than it had ever been before.

But at the same time, my life was suddenly harder than it had ever been before. Internally, I felt a new kind of conviction and sorrow over my sins and failures. I felt twisted and pulled in two directions, as part of me desperately wanted to follow Jesus, but another part of me was still drawn to sin. When I saw other people suffering, I hurt with them and for them in a new way. Many days, my heart felt like a jumbled mess of joy and sorrow, peace and pain, hope and discouragement.

Externally, things were hard as well. As I started sharing the great news of my new relationship with Jesus with my friends and family members, very few of them were as excited as I was about Jesus. Some of them were pretty freaked out. A few of them said hurtful and discouraging things to me, even accusing me of being a fanatic and a cult member. There were times where I had to separate myself from friends who were making destructive decisions and expecting me to do the same. Some of those friends made fun of me and tried to embarrass me in front of others. There were times where I felt rejected and alone and it hurt. I found myself wondering and even saying to God, "I gave my life to Jesus, why is my life so hard?"

My guess is, that if you are a follower of Jesus, then you can relate to much of my story. You have received Jesus in faith. You have turned from your sins and turned your life over to Jesus. You love Jesus and you are so thankful for his love for you. But life is still hard. You still struggle with sin. You still get sick. People still fail you and betray you. You gave your life to Jesus, but life is hard, maybe even harder than it was before you became a Christian. You may be struggling with doubt, wondering if following Jesus is really worth it. You may be tempted to give up, to turn back to your old life and walk away from Jesus. You may feel like Jesus has failed you. Given up on you. Turned away from you. You may be losing hope. What should you do? How should you move forward? How can you continue to love and follow Jesus even when life is really hard? Let me share a couple of things with you that I believe will help you, encourage you, and strengthen you as you seek to follow Jesus.

Recognize where you are.

One of the things that I love most about Jesus is his honesty. Jesus never lies. He is always straightforward and clear in the ways that he describes what it really means to be one of his disciples. In the Gospel of John, chapter 16, Jesus is honest and straightforward about the pain and hardship that his followers should expect: "In this world, you will have tribulation" (John 16:33). In other words, Jesus is saying, "You are going to experience trials. You are going to suffer. You are going to have trouble. Life is going to be hard." Jesus wants us to recognize that in the world in which we live, even as his followers, life will be hard.

God's Word tells us that life is hard for a variety of reasons. First, life is hard because our world is broken. Part of God's good judgment against our sin is a curse on this present world (Genesis 3:16-19). Things like earthquakes, and cancer, and job layoffs were not a part of God's original design for us or for his world. God allows and causes these hard things to happen in the world and in our lives because of his judgment against sin.

This broken world is also filled with broken people, who live in sinful rebellion against God. As we seek to walk with Jesus, we will be constantly walking against the flow of many of our friends, neighbors and family members. We will constantly experience the difficulty and pain that comes from people who are running away from God bumping into us, crashing into us, and trying to pull us away from Jesus.

One day, when Jesus comes back to remake and restore this broken world, there will be no more hard things and no more sad things. But, until that great day comes, we will continue to follow Jesus in a broken world. And because our world is broken, life is hard.

Second, life is hard because our hearts are sinful. The great news for us is that when we receive Jesus in faith, God graciously saves us from death and gives us new life (Ephesians 2:1-10). He also mercifully frees us from the penalty of our sin (Romans 3:23-26). By the power and work of the Holy Spirit, God begins a process of transforming us to make us more and more like Jesus that will ultimately end in glory (Romans 8:28-30). And yet, right now the hard reality is that until we see Jesus face-to-face on the other side of death, or when he returns to earth, the presence of sin will remain in our hearts. Jesus has freed us from the penalty of our sins and the Holy Spirit is freeing us from the power of sin, but we will battle against the presence of sin our entire lives. The Apostle Paul describes this vividly in chapter 7 of the Book of Romans:

> For I do not understand my own actions. For I do not do what I want, but I do the very thing I hate…I have the desire to do what is right, but not the ability to carry it out. For I do not do the good I want, but the evil I do not want is what I keep on doing…when I want to do right, evil lies close at hand. For I delight in the law of God in my inner being, but I see in my members another law waging war against the law of my mind and making me captive to the law of sin that dwells in my members. Wretched man that I am! Who will deliver me from this body of death? (Romans 7:15, 18-19, 21-24).

In these verses, Paul describes our struggle against sin as a war. War is violent. War is painful. War is hard. And as we seek to follow Jesus, life will be hard as our sinful nature wars against the Spirit in us and as we make war against our sin.

Finally, life is hard because we have an enemy. Satan is real and he hates God and he wants to do everything he can to shut down God's work in God's people. As we seek to follow Jesus, God tells us in his Word that Satan is like a lion, looking for opportunities to destroy us and demolish us: "Your adversary the devil prowls around like a roaring lion, seeking someone to devour" (1 Peter 5:8). Satan's attacks come at us through distractions, deceptions and temptations.

Satan and his demons are violently opposed to God's gracious work in our lives. Mez McConnell says it like this:

> All the enemies of God are violently opposed to us. Not only do they seek to tear us away from Jesus. But they want one of His enemies to reign over us in His place. From the first moment we are saved in Christ, war has been declared against us by those who want us to give up on Christ and go back to our old way of living. Unlike a game that comes to an end within hours, they will try and oppose our commitment to Jesus until the day we die.[1]

Life is hard because we live in a broken world. Life is hard because our hearts are sinful. Life is hard because we have an enemy. Jesus does not want us to surprised or taken off guard by these things. He does not want us to live with unrealistic expectations of a trouble-free life. He wants us to know what to expect so that we can be prepared; so that we can be ready; so that we will know what to do when trouble comes and life gets hard; and so that we will respond to the hard things in our lives in the best possible way. And how should we respond? What should we do when life is hard?

Remember who Jesus is.

In the second part of John 16:33, after Jesus tells us that we will experience tribulation and trouble, he tells us that in the midst of those tribulations and trouble, we should remember who he is: "In this world, you will have tribulation. *But take heart; I have overcome the world*" (emphasis mine). Do you see what he says there? First, he says, "take heart." In other words, be encouraged, have hope, be bold and confident, don't give up, and be courageous. Jesus says that in the face of the hard things we experience, we should take heart. But why?

Because of the second thing he says: "I have overcome the world." In other words, Jesus is saying, "Take heart. Be encouraged.

Be bold and confident and don't give up as you experience trouble and hard times because I have triumphed over those troubles. I have defeated those hard things. I have conquered those enemies." We can walk through hard times with full hearts because Jesus has overcome.

Here is how he did it: through his perfect life, sacrificial death, and victorious resurrection. When Jesus came and lived without sin, died on the cross for our sin, and rose from the grace to defeat sin, Satan, and death, he overcame and won the ultimate battle for us. In Colossians 2:15, it says, "He (Jesus) disarmed the rulers and authorities and put them to open shame, by triumphing over them in him." In the midst of the tribulations and trouble and hard things you will experience in this world, you can take heart, have courage, and choose hope because Jesus has overcome the world.

Here is the truth: we will either be overcome by the hard things and the troubles we experience in this world, or with Jesus' help, we will overcome. Every follower of Jesus is either overcome or is an overcomer. The world wants to overcome us…and it is relentless. Our sinful heart wants to overcome us…and it is relentless. Satan wants to overcome us…and he is relentless.

But listen…we don't have to be overcome by these things. No, we can be overcomers because we belong to God and we are connected to the One who has already overcome all of these things! Jesus is THE Overcomer! Through his life, death, and resurrection he has overcome all of the hard things and difficult trouble we could ever possibly experience.

And check this out: one day, when Jesus returns to rule and reign here on earth, he is going to put an end to all of the hard things, forever. No more broken world. No more sinful hearts. No more attacks from Satan and his demons. When he comes again, Jesus will finally and fully put an end to all of the trouble and hard things we have experienced in this life. He will restore our broken world. He will remake our sinful hearts. He will destroy Satan and his demons. He will triumph over all of our troubles and we will only experience his perfect love and perfect joy for all eternity. Here is how God describes that incredible day:

> Then I saw a new heaven and a new earth, for the first heaven and the first earth had passed away, and the sea was no more. And I saw the holy city, new Jerusalem, coming down out of heaven from God, prepared as a bride adorned for her husband. And I heard a loud voice from the throne saying, "Behold, the dwelling place of God is with man. He will dwell with them, and they will be his people, and God himself will be with them as their God. He will wipe away every tear from their eyes, and death shall be no more, neither shall there be any mourning, nor crying, nor pain anymore, for the former things have passed away" (Revelation 21:1-4).

Here is an amazing truth that will give you courage to walk with Jesus through hard things until Jesus comes again: this overcoming, victorious, triumphing-over-trouble Jesus is totally *for you*. Psalm 56:9 says, "This I know, that God is for me." Read that verse again. Slowly. "This…I know…that…God… is… for…me." Not against me. Not neutrally "ok" with me. No…He is for me! This means that in every aspect of every area of my everyday life, God is actively working for my good. He is working for my joy. He is working for my hope. He is working for my flourishing. He is working for my marriage. He is working for my family. He is working for my career. He is at work *for me*. The living God of all power and grace and love and holiness is *for me*. Totally. Completely. Perfectly. For. Me.

And because God is for me, he is completely committed and completely capable of working through all of the hard things I experience to do good things in me. He can take my sufferings and use them to grow my joy. He can use the attacks of my enemies to give me a greater experience of his love. He will work in the middle of my worst physical sickness to deepen my spiritual strength. God will use all the hard things in my life to accomplish even more good things in my heart. The Apostle Paul says it like this: "And we know that for those who love God all things work together for good, for those who are called according to his purpose" (Romans 8:28). Did you catch that? *All things* will work together for my good. The "all things" of this verse includes good and happy things and hard and sad things. "All things" means all things, including the suffering and trouble we experience as we follow Jesus in this broken world.

God's promise to work all things together for our good doesn't mean that things will always go the way we want. Or that we won't lose, won't suffer, or won't face difficult circumstances. We will. Remember, Jesus promised that in this life, as his people, we will experience trouble.

But here is what it does mean: God will use every awful, horrible, hard thing that we experience to give us a greater and more wonderful experience of knowing Jesus, enjoying Jesus, and becoming more and more like Jesus. As you go through hard times, remember that in every prayer that isn't answered the way you want, in every loss, in every suffering, and in every attack from every enemy that is totally against you, Jesus has overcome the world, he is for totally for you, and he will use every hard thing in your life to give you wonderful joy forever.

DISCUSSION QUESTIONS

1. How has your life changed since beginning to walk with Jesus? How has your perspective changed?

2. How does recognizing the truth of where we are, in this life, help us to stay steady during hard times?

3. Think back to a hard time in your life. What good things did God accomplish in your heart during that time?

Chapter 12

WHY DOES GOD CARE ABOUT MY SEX LIFE?

Evan Skelton

> But sexual immorality and all impurity or covetousness must not even be named among you, as is proper among saints. Let there be no filthiness nor foolish talk nor crude joking, which are out of place, but instead let there be thanksgiving. For you may be sure of this, that everyone who is sexually immoral or impure, or who is covetous (that is, an idolater), has no inheritance in the kingdom of Christ and God. Let no one deceive you with empty words, for because of these things the wrath of God comes upon the sons of disobedience. Therefore do not become partners with them; (Ephesians 5:3–7).

I used to teach Jr. High Boys as a Bible teacher, and I used to use something we called "the Question Jar" into which they could put any question they had, and if we had time before class was done, I'd draw one or two out to answer. Can you guess what the number one topic they wanted to talk about was?

Sex.

We are not so different from Jr. High boys. We love talking about sex as a culture. But the conversation quickly gets... well... complicated, doesn't it? Just think about how many of our current cultural battles are about sex, and how many are around the corner still.

Some reading this are excited by the revolutions occurring now on a global scale, even proud to see a world which does not question who you love or how you identify. Even while we're certain the Bible has opinions on our sex lives, we're not so sure we even to hear what the church has to say, especially if it would join with those standing in the way of progress, tied to their dusty even repressive traditionalism.

Others of us, however, are fairly certain the world is now going into hell in a handbasket, in large part for how we have compromised around sexuality and its expression. We aren't so sure we should be talking about sex in public, but we'll put up with it so long as the pastor lets *those* people, whoever they might be, know they are in the wrong.

It is no wonder many Christians avoid what the Bible says about sexuality or at least spend so much of their clarifying so much of what they *don't* mean that it is difficult to know what they *do* mean. The door is so often slammed before even before the conversation even starts.

Perhaps the reason this conversation awakens diverse and intense emotions from us is because we rightly sense the conversation is actually about something much deeper, something which pricks our nervous centers, exposing some of the most basic questions we ask about ourselves.

This, I would argue, is exactly why sex is not a subject which should be merely reserved for hushed conversations and private bedroom commitments. And this is why Christians should be more frank and clear about what God has to say about our sexuality than ever before. Because our sex lives have a lot more to do with more than how we *identify*. It has to do with our *identity*.

Two Narratives

I used to be a youth pastor, and let me tell you, the room I inherited was a piece of work—moldy couches, holes in the drywall, and one wall where every student had at one point years before I got there signed their name in permanent marker.

Now, have you ever tried to paint over permanent marker? We tried. And then we tried again. And again. But every time, you know what happened? The marker bled to the surface.

Unfortunately, sometimes confessing Christians out of fear or disdain for what they cannot relate with, have be murderous with their words, perhaps with you. Some of the most painful words and even blows you have received in your whole life may have come from those who claimed to follow Christ.

But still, have you ever wondered why so many *other* Christians so apparently kind and understanding, so absent of self-righteousness and cruelty, insist on drawing the line here? Why do they and the God they confess care so much about what takes place behind closed doors between consenting adults?

Why can't what v. 11 calls "what is done in secret" remain there? Why can't we live and let live? In short, why does God care about my sex life?

What can be misleading about our current debates is that the issue, at least for the biblically-minded Christian *is not*, at least fundamentally, about sexuality and its expression. In fact, though the issues have been layered one upon another, the line we see in the Bible is one that has in a sense "bled through the layers," a line which has been drawn at a much deeper and more fundamental level. The line, in fact, has to do with two competing narratives by which we make sense of our lives, two ways of seeing the world which humans have warred over for much longer than the last twenty years.

Narrative #1. Fulfillment is found in self-seeking.

The first narrative says that fulfillment is self-made. Fulfillment is found in self-seeking. You can hear it in our most basic cultural proverbs–"Follow your heart," "Find your own way," "Be true to yourself." It's as common place as Disney. Just listen to these lines from *Moana*:

> *And the call isn't out there at all*
> *It's inside me*
> *…*
> *You'll remind me*
> *That come what may, I know the way*
> *I am Moana!*

The first narrative says that I have not only the right but the *duty* to stay true to myself. It is my only hope for finding happiness. I must be free to be me! This is exactly WHY the fight for sexual expression even for a woman's right to chose an abortion seems of such pressing importance to some of us, why it seems to be no less than a justice issue. I must be free to be me!

What is our supreme value? Authenticity. What is our primary ethic? Consent. We argue that a person should be free to love, identify, and explore so long as it brings them closer to happiness and doesn't harm anyone else. This is the meaning of life, in fact— to make or discover my own meaning—and I must be free to do so on my terms. To disagree or deny me that life is the definition of oppression.

Even in popular culture, the fight for sexual freedom is about so much more than the right to use my body how I want.

Narrative #2. Fulfillment is found in self-denial.

The Bible, however, offers not just an alternative way of seeing the world. It stands this narrative on its head. Just listen to Jesus' words in Matthew 16:

> Then Jesus told his disciples, "If anyone would come after me, let him deny himself and take up his cross and follow me. For whoever would save his life will lose it, but whoever loses his life for my sake will find it.

According to Jesus, fulfillment is not found in self-seeking but in *self-denial*. Fulfillment is not found in fighting for your passions but in denying many desires which feel all too natural, refusing to let my body have the final say.

It turns out this offends everyone, whether you agree with a biblical sexuality or not. We all have desires we don't want to deny, avoiding the path of the cross at all costs. And this, we will come to see next, makes us all sexually broken, sometimes especially those in committed heterosexual relationships.

3 Questions

Question #1: What must we deny?

Now the Bible uses several words for our sexual brokenness, many of which we see in the text I quoted at the beginning of this chapter—"sexual immorality… impurity… filthiness… foolish talk… course joking" (Ephesians 1:1-7).

This barrage of words summarizes the spectrum of speech and actions which divert from God's created intent for sex—a life-long faithful marriage between a man and a women. It includes sleeping around but also pornography. It includes homosexual sex but also heterosexual affairs. It includes back-alley rape but also locker-room humor. It includes "taking him to bed" but also "checking her out."

These terms include anything that threatens, discards, or mocks the profound union of marriage.

But, standing out from this list is one vice which doesn't immediately appear to belong. In fact, it is repeated twice: *"covetousness/envy"* (v. 3, 5). Why? What is the essence of envy? Envy is the desire for what doesn't belong to me, a controlling desire for fulfillment on the other side of the fence. In fact, in a sense, envy makes a god out of the thing it desires.

You see, the reason we sin is not merely because we stepped out of line, or even because we desire the object or person in front of us. We sin because we have made them our god, our means to ultimate security, pleasure, identity. We have made a person or object our means to ultimate fulfillment. This is why Paul calls it "idolatry" (v. 5).

The problem with the gods we make whether out of boyfriends or pixels on a screen is that idolatry turns a person, even those we love, into a means. Every time. Idolatry says with Jerry McGuire: *"You complete me,"* looking to our relationships to make us whole. But no relationship can bear this weight, and it turns people into a means for my own self-interest. After all, how many of you have been in love only to be discarded after your lover got what they wanted? Or punished your spouse by withholding sex? Or broken things off because they no longer held up their end of the bargain? Idolatry uses people.

But more importantly, idols can't be satisfied. They can't deliver on what they promise. The satisfaction we need goes far deeper than what the best lover can provide. How many have had your dreams come true only to wonder if you made the wrong choice? If you can stand being stuck with this person till death do you part? How long is before you begin wonder to yourself, "if only my husband talked to me the way he does?" or "if my girlfriend looked like she did?"

Or, let's use the multi-billion dollar industry of pornography. Of all the men and women I know who have struggled with it, I don't know of anyone who has ever reached the point where they have said, "Wow. I feel like that last video or picture was enough for me. Moving on." Have you ever been shocked at how much further your daydreams or late nights have gone than you ever thought they would?

We are all sexually broken, not only in our actions, but more fundamentally in our desires. Looking to wring out something from our sexuality that it simply cannot give. The acts matter, but the *reason* we sin this way so naturally and so frequently is because of a desire underneath the desire, a counterfeit god showing its face in the women or men we use. And like a bug bite which itches more as you scratch it, the envy is insatiable.

Again, we are all sexually broken, not only in our actions, but more fundamentally in our desires.

Question #2: Why must we deny?

One used to hear a lot about the search for a "gay gene," and we may again. It was thought that if we could find a genetic link for who we are attracted to, proof that it is in our basic wiring, then that would eradicate any notion that acting on such attraction was unfit. In fact, some of our most popular songs, like "Born This Way" by Lady Gaga celebrated this notion.

Today, however, you don't hear much about this search. Instead, in many circles it is deeply offensive now to say someone is "born this way." It's heresy, in fact. In light of the gender revolution, it is instead argued that what matters is not genes but *instinct*. It is not something you find out in a lab but feel in your gut. Identity according to many can fluctuate moment to moment.

As a result, even secular psychologists have expressed concern that we are not getting to a more stable sense of self as a culture but more unstable. We're becoming more fractured, more insecure and frenetic.

When the Bible uses the language that sexual indiscretion is "not proper" or "out of place." He doesn't just mean that it breaks a rule. The reason it is not proper is that our sexual identity is an insufficient place to root our sense of self. According to the Bible, this is because our identities are meant to be rooted in something more fundamental than even our sexuality. Our identities, in fact, come from a love relationship, but a love relationship with God himself.[1]

This means that marriage and sex within marriage, looks *beyond* itself. It plays out the disclosure, the commitment, and the union which are finally made to be expressed between human beings and God himself. In fact, every love relationship, in a sense, is made to look beyond itself, and our haunting sense of longing goes far beyond the person in front of us. And our longing will continue to both crave and grieve until it sees the one in whom our soul will truly delight—God himself.

We deny ourselves in light of our present identity, but it would be unwise to leave it here, because the Bible also says we must deny in light of "coming judgement.: The Bible paints the picture very honestly. Those who persist not only in sexual immorality but also in the idolatry underneath can't expect to inherit God's new world. Instead, they await the anger of *the* betrayed lover and its consequences, the anger of God himself.

And yet, I need to say a word of comfort to those of us who are shrinking in our chair as we read this. Some of us are certain that if God is going to rescue anyone, it surely isn't us. Our lives our too broken. "If these he only knew who I was, what I have done, or what I am now even doing, he wouldn't give me the time of day."

But, there is only one "hopeless case" in God's eyes, and that is the one who will not admit that they are among the sick and come to the doctor for life. The threat of the Bible is not for those who are worse off than they ever dared admit[2] but for those who will not admit.

Among God's people, you are not going to find the put together but the falling apart. You won't find the spotless but the stained. You won't find "big shots" but beggars pointing one another to the bread. And, everyone who confesses their brokenness, no matter what baggage you bring along, and turns in faith to Jesus will be wrapped in clean robes of righteousness. They will be finally declared as pure, not soiled…whole, not broken… loved, not discarded. Because in Jesus, they are indeed.

This brings us to our third and final question.

Question #3: How can we deny?

One of the most moving pictures of what we are talking about here comes from the memoirs of Jackie Hill Perry. In her book, *Gay Girl Good God,* Jackie describes her experience of gender confusion and her once whole-hearted embrace of homosexuality, something which she says felt more natural to her than heterosexuality ever could. But more importantly, she describes came to find the wholeness she was seeking in Jesus.

Early on in the book, she describes the day *after* she came to faith in Christ, in which a beautiful young woman entered the checkout line where she worked, and like clockwork desire rose up in her. "But," she recounts, "I also wanted something else: God."

> Wanting God over a woman was an entirely new experience for me. It wasn't even something I considered as being a part of Christianity, let alone the Christian. It seemed to be a religion of just duty. I've met so many disciples who preached more of sin than joy, whose eyes were stuck in a constant state of solemnity, clenched teeth and an endless fascination with holiness. Why

haven't they ever mentioned the place happiness had within righteousness, or how the taking up of the cross would be a practice of obtaining delight? Delight in all that God is? Even their saviour had this kind of joy in mind as he endured his cross. So why haven't they set their focus on the same? In their defence, they were not to blame for my unbelief. I just wonder if they would have told me about the beauty of God just as much, if not more, than they told me about the horridness of hell, if I would have burned my idols at a faster place.[3]

Yes, Jackie would say that coming to Christ soon necessitated fighting rather than giving in to her desires. It required a kind of self-denial which, at times, felt a lot like death. But what enabled her and enables us to deny the desires which feel so natural to us is the fulfillment found in Christ alone. Jackie continues:

In my becoming holy as he is, I would not be miraculously made into a woman that didn't like women; I would be made into a woman that loved God more than anything.

You see friends, this is the hope which self-denial offers that self-seeking is just not capable of. In the end, according to Jesus, fulfillment is not something I make. Fulfillment is something I receive.

Going back to Jesus' words in Matthew 16, loss comes to all who seek to make their own fulfillment, who allow their bodies to have the final say, even ultimate loss. But the promise for those who die to themselves in the thousand tiny deaths of self-sacrifice, those who entrust their fulfillment to God instead of themselves, those who lose their lives… will find them.

Why does God care?

Why does God care about my sex life? Because he cares about my joy. Because he cares about my fulfillment. We will only taste this delight if we deny ourselves. But at a more fundamental level, we only have this delight, because on the cross, Christ denied himself first, more ultimately and willingly than we ever could. And out of the joy set before him, he secured at infinite cost a kind of delight our sexuality could never provide.

Because of this self-denying love, there is nothing this life can keep back from you that is not already yours in him. You no longer need to demand. You can give. You no longer need to be suffocated in envy. You can breathe deep with contentment. You don't need to seek after your life in self-made gods, for you have found your life in the God who gave his own.

> ### DISCUSSION QUESTIONS
>
> 1. How do you see the narrative "Fulfillment is found in self-seeking," at work in our present cultural climate?
>
> 2. Do you agree that we are all sexually broken? Why or why not?
>
> 3. Why is it necessary to identify the desires underneath our actions? What happens if we do not?
>
> 4. What do you think the author means when he says, "The threat of the Bible is not for those who are worse off than they ever dared admit but for those who will not admit."
>
> 5. How does Jackie Hill Perry's story help you understand Jesus' words in Matthew 16:25: "For whoever would save his life will lose it, but whoever loses his life for my sake will find it"?

Chapter 13

HOW CAN I BE MORE CHRIST-LIKE IN MY COMMUNICATION?

Jordan Branch

If you are a Christian, you are God's child (1 John 3:2). Just as children imitate the behavior of their parents, God wants his adopted children to imitate him (Ephesians 5:1–2). In the Apostle Paul's letter to the church in Ephesus, he says imitating God looks like someone changing clothes. Like we replace our old clothes with new clothes, we need to replace our sinful emotions and behaviors with emotions that reflect our newfound relationship with God through Jesus Christ. We do this in the context of relationships with others (Ephesians 4:17–24). As we submit, seek, savor, and serve our God in the context of everyday relationships, he renews us to become more and more like Jesus (Ephesians 4:23). This is good news for us, for no one had more joy and peace in imitating God the Father than God the Son! In Ephesians 4:25–32, the Apostle Paul provides five ways we replace our sinful communication with God-imitating communication.

1. Replace lying with truth-telling.

> Therefore, having put away falsehood let each one of you speak the truth with his neighbor, for we are members one of another (Ephesians 4:25).

God desires that all Christians present the truth to others in love (Proverbs 12:22; Ephesians 4:15). False words affect the whole church. If we want unity in our relationships, we must be honest. For a relationship to grow and deepen, there must be trust.

This practice of truth telling is ultimately a reflection of God. Unlike the lies of Satan, God always tells the truth. In everything he does, he is always honest and truthful. Our honesty and truthfulness in relationships reflects the character of our God, who is also honest and truthful in everything he does (Numbers 23:19). We grow more like our God and we grow closer together when we tell the truth.

2. Replace unrighteous anger with righteous anger.

> Be angry and do not sin; do not let the sun go down on your anger, and give no opportunity to the devil (Ephesians 4:26–27).

Anger is a universal problem, prevalent in every culture, and experienced by every generation. Anger can take different forms in different people. Robert Jones writes, "Whether you tend to simmer or strike out, whether you implode or explode, there is biblical help for you. Jesus died and rose to help you uproot ungodly anger."[1] We can replace unrighteous anger with godliness and righteous anger.

Our anger arises from our perception of the injustice committed against us or others. We should have righteous anger when we see injustice toward God's Kingdom. We should love what God loves and hate what God hates (Psalm 119:53). We know anger as righteous rather than sinful when it is accompanied by other godly qualities and expresses itself in godly ways.

To replace unrighteous anger with righteous anger, we first need to uproot sinful anger. Think of a time when you were angry. What happened? What concern, or right did you perceive as being unjust or unfair either to you or others? So often we get angry when we do not get something we deeply want. Jesus tells us sinful anger arises from the sinful beliefs and motives in our hearts.

> What comes out of a person is what defiles him. For from within, out of the heart of man, come evil thoughts, sexual immorality, theft, murder, adultery, coveting, wickedness, deceit, sensuality, envy, slander, pride, foolishness. All these evil things come from within, and they defile a person (Mark 7:20).

The biblical term *heart* refers to a person's inner self, one's thoughts, will, affections, and emotions.

You and I will always have things we want deeply. We want respect, appreciation, gratitude, love, intimacy, comfort, friendship, support, equality, obedience, etc. Sinful and unrighteous anger often surfaces when these deep desires remain unmet. Listen to what James says:

> What causes quarrels and what causes fights among you? Is it not this, that your *passions* are at war within you? You *desire* and do not have, so you murder. You covet and cannot obtain, so you fight and quarrel (James 4:1-2).

Our sinful & unrighteous anger (quarrels and fighting) comes from unmet desires that *rule* our hearts. The deep roots of anger often reveal that we want good things more than we want the best thing—God himself. God is the rightful ruler of our life, and he should be the greatest desire of our heart.

Here is good news: God's grace can reach the depths of our inordinate and ruling desires and change our hearts. Give your unmet desires to the Lord (Psalm 55:22). Repent and ask God to make him your greatest desire and love (Mark 12:30). Take joy in knowing that our gracious God has fully forgiven you (1 John 1:9). Believe in the liberating and freeing promises of the gospel for angry people (2 Peter 1:3).

3. Replace stealing with working and giving.

> Let the thief no longer steal, but rather let him labor, doing honest work with his own hands, so that he may have something to share with anyone in need (Ephesians 4:28).

God commands us not to steal (Exodus 20:15), but rather to focus on the needs of others. The goal of working rather than stealing is to give to others in need. We are to replace stealing, theft and cheating with working and giving. God calls us to love our neighbor as our self (Mark 12:31) and to consider others better than our self (Philippians 2:3). Either we can work to get for ourselves, or we can work in order to give to others.

Christians have a new identity, don't we? When we find our identity and joy in Christ, we are free to live differently! When we believe that in Christ God has provided for us more satisfying promises for comfort and security then we are free to give and to give generously in proportion to what we have (Philippians 4:19; Hebrews 13:5–6). As we seek to be more God glorifying in our communication, it will allow our words to give life to people as we speak, instead of stealing life and joy with our words.

4. Replace corrupt talk with edifying talk.

> Let no corrupting talk come out of your mouths, but only such as is good for building up, as fits the occasion, that it may give grace to those who hear. And do not grieve the Holy Spirit of God, by whom you were sealed for the day of redemption (Ephesians 4:29–30).

Do you build others up with your speech or do you tear others down? Are you prone to cynicism and negativity or encouragement and grace? As Christians, we must replace corrupt talk like gossip, slander, and cynicism with edifying, encouraging, and grace-filled talk. If you struggle with giving grace in your communication with others, remember the direct connection between how we speak and the condition of our hearts (Luke 6:43–45).

All of us in some form or another have been on the receiving end of corrupt speech. We often form our identity and attitudes by the corrupt talk of others. How we speak to others reveals the depth of our belief in the gospel. Giving grace and making peace reveals the power of God's grace at work in our hearts to restore our true identity as children of God.

The gospel gives us a new and better identity than the negative pictures others paint of us with their words. Reading the first part of Paul's letter to the Ephesians helps us understand this. Paul says in Christ we are chosen and adopted by the Father (1:4–6), redeemed by the Son (1:7–12), sealed with the Spirit (1:13–14), brought from death to life by grace through faith in Christ (2:1–10), and created for good works which God has prepared for us (2:10). The more and more we believe these truths in our life, the more they change us from the inside out replacing corrupt talk with edifying talk. As we fill our hearts with truths of God's grace, it fills and transforms our hearts, overflowing until we become more and more grace-giving with our words.

5. Replace bitterness and rage with kindness and forgiveness.

> Let all bitterness and wrath and anger and clamor and slander be put away from you, along with all malice. Be kind to one another, tenderhearted, forgiving one another, as God in Christ forgave you (Ephesians 4:31–32).

Christian, God calls you to replace resentful attitudes and behaviors like bitterness, anger, slander, and hostility. Instead we are to be a people characterized by kindness, compassion, and forgiveness. When we love others this way, we reflect the character of God (see Exodus 34:6).

Learning to demonstrate kindness and grant forgiveness can be some of the most difficult things you ever do. It may seem easy, but it is not. C.S. Lewis once said "Everyone thinks forgiveness is a lovely idea, until he has something to forgive."[2] Friend, remember your forgiveness from God in Jesus Christ. Remember how much he has forgiven you (Luke 7:47)! When you doubt whether you should give love, kindness, or forgiveness to your offender, remember the demonstrated love of God for you in Jesus Christ. "…but God shows his love for us in that while we were still sinners, Christ died for us" (Romans 5:8).

The strength to love and forgive the unkind, the offensive, and the hateful comes in increasing measure, as we understand and experience the extent of God's forgiveness to us. How grateful are you for Jesus's death on your behalf? The power of gratefulness grows in our hearts when we understand more and more God's holiness and our sinfulness. Your God has died for you so that you could be forgiven! Over 250 years ago, a new Christian named Charles Wesley wrote a song expressing his amazement of God's love for him in the death of Jesus Christ. Wesley wrote, "Amazing love! How can it be that thou, my God, should die for me!"[3] Christian, pray for God to increase your wonder, joy, and gratitude for Jesus death on the cross for you. As God has forgiven you, forgive, love, and show kindness to others. If Jesus can forgive us, then there is nothing for which should not forgive another person.

DISCUSSION QUESTIONS

1. How has your communication changed since you became a follower of Christ?

2. How does our increasing understanding of the Gospel impact our communication?

3. As you reflect on these five ways to replace your sinful communication with God-imitating communication, which one does God want to change in you?

Chapter 14

HOW CAN I IMPROVE MY PRAYER LIFE?

Dave Herre

> I feel sure that as long as we look on prayer chiefly as the means of maintaining our own Christian life, we shall not know fully what it is meant to be. But when we learn to regard it as the highest part of the work entrusted to us, the root and strength of all other work, we shall see that there is nothing that we so need to study and practice as the art of praying aright.
>
> – Andrew Murray

As I read through and study a passage of Scripture, I like to ask the question, "What does this passage tell me about the character of God?" The answer often is that we have a God who speaks and reveals himself to us. And yet, he is also the God who calls us to speak to him! God is not disinterested and uninvolved with us, his creation. He calls us into relationship as he reveals himself to us and calls us into conversation as we respond in prayer. Prayer is an amazing gift to us that speaks much of the character of our God and his love for us.

What is prayer?

Simply, prayer is our active communication with God. This may be a voiced prayer (Psalms 18:6), silent prayer in the quiet of our soul (Matt 6:6), groaning of inner struggles to God that are beyond words (Psalms 5:1; Romans 8:26) and prayers voiced and agreed upon with other followers of Jesus (Acts 1:14; 2:42).

R.C. Sproul in his book *Essential Truths of the Christian Faith* helps us further our understanding of prayer:

> We commune with [God] through prayer. Charles Hodge declared that "prayer is the converse of the soul with God." In and through prayer we express our reverence and adoration for God; we bare our souls in contrite confession before Him; we pour out the thanksgiving of grateful hearts; and we offer our petitions and supplication to Him.[1]

Prayer is a conduit of God's grace that he uses to pour out his unfailing love, his grace, his mercy, his strength and his presence. It is not a mere method of maintaining our walk with Jesus, it is at the root and foundation of our relationship with him. We must treasure prayer as an essential element in our relationship with God just as breathing is to our physical life. And yet, we do struggle to pray and must look to God's Word to teach us to pray and call upon the strength of God to help us.

Why do we pray?

First, our prayer to God is an act of faithful obedience to his Word. We see a call to prayer in the New Testament writings of Paul to the early churches when he writes, "Devote yourselves to prayer, stay alert in it with thanksgiving" (Colossians 4:2) and, "Pray constantly" (1 Thessalonians 5:17). It is God's plan for us, his children, to continually speak to him our praises, needs, struggles, confessions, and thanksgivings. We pray to him therefore, in faithful obedience knowing his plans and commands given to us are for our good!

Second, we pray because our God invites us to pray and enter into deeper fellowship with him. When Jesus' disciples saw his practice of frequent prayer they came to him and requested, "Lord, teach us to pray." Jesus responds by saying, "When you pray, say: Father..." and he began teaching them what often is referred to as the Lord's Prayer (Luke 11:1-2). We can look to this prayer as an invitation to pray to our Heavenly Father. "For the Lord's Prayer is not so much a command as an invitation: an invitation to share in the prayer-life of Jesus himself."[2]

A final reason we pray is not because God is uninformed about our situation, our thoughts, our trials, or even our joys, but because our prayer is an expression of our trust in him alone (Matt 6:8-9).

> God wants us to pray because prayer expresses our trust in God and is a means whereby our trust in him can increase. In fact, perhaps the primary emphasis of the Bible's teaching on prayer is that we are to pray with faith, which means trust or dependence on God.[3]

Throughout the New Testament we are taught to pray with faith, with our trust placed in God alone (Luke 11:9-13; Matt 21:22; Mark 11:24; 1 Peter 5:6-7; Phil 4:6-6; James 1:6-8; 5:14-15). We are to cast our burdens and worries upon God who is more than able to carry them (1 Peter 5:1). Prayer is an active demonstration of our trust in God and not in ourselves. So, pray trusting and resting in God who is able to hear and answer for our good and his great glory!

How do we pray?

You may be wondering, "Do I need to pray on my knees? Can I pray standing with my hands raised? Can I pray with loud shouts or just in the silence of my heart? Do my eyes need to be closed? What if I am driving?" There are many postures (kneeling, standing, walking, etc.), circumstances, and scenarios in which we can and must pray but most important is the posture of our heart when we pray. We should pray, with humble reverence and faith, to God who is our audience (Matthew 6:9; Psalm 34:4-6, 50:15). As a poor man with empty, open hands we pray, and he hears and saves us out of our trials (Psalm 34:5). Often there are times that we come to God in our sadness, joy, grief, fear, confusion, and anger. Yet our prayer should begin with a recognition of our great need and of our mighty God who is able to hear, answer, and provide. 1 Peter 5:5b-7 says:

> God opposes the proud but gives grace to the humble. Humble yourselves, therefore, under the mighty hand of God so that at the proper time he may exalt you, casting all your anxieties on him, because he cares for you.

In Matthew 6:5-6, Jesus teaches his disciples about the humble posture of prayer which is to be made to the audience of God alone. We are not to pray with the purpose of demonstrating to others how spiritual we are. He warns those who might be tempted to stand on street corners praying so that they can been seen by others. In contrast, Jesus calls his disciples to begin their prayer in private before God alone. If it is done for the praise of man, you may receive their praise but that is all you will get, it will not satisfy (Matthew 5:6). So, find a time and place that you can regularly go to be alone and speak to God. If our prayer is out of humble faith, our prayer will begin in secret before God alone.

The question might be asked, can we pray in public? Yes, we can pray in public as we gather with others. We see public prayer demonstrated in the early church as they met together (Acts 1:14; 2:42; 4:31; 12:5). Nonetheless, we must be reminded that God is the One to whom we pray. "We should never utter one syllable of prayer, either in public or in private, until we are definitely conscious that we have come into the presence of God and are actually praying to him."4

What do we pray?

You might also ask, "What words can I use?" As we pray, there is not a magic formula or special vocabulary we have to use to make ourselves heard by God. Instead we come with humble confidence in prayer through our Mediator Jesus. Our Mediator died in our place, rose from the grave victorious over sin and death so that we can come freely to God (2 Corinthians 5:21; Romans 5:1-2; 8:1; Hebrews 4:14-16). Nonetheless, Jesus does give his disciples a guide to help them (and us) know what to pray in the Lord's Prayer.

#1. Jesus teaches that when we pray, we are to have a Godward focus.

Instead of focusing on our needs and desires, we begin by directing our heart, words, and attention to God. Jesus begins his prayer, "Our Father in heaven..." We are to address God in a very personal manner, as a child to a father. This is a call to come to God in prayer without fear of rejection. We are adopted sons and daughters who can enter directly into prayer with our Heavenly Father.

After addressing God as Father, Jesus' prayer follows with praise to God by praying, "...hallowed be your name." This is a prayer that peoples near and far will worship and give praise and honor to God. Our prayers should begin with acknowledgement of God and his holiness. We give our Father praise in response to who he is as well as thanksgiving for what he has done and will do.

Then he prays, "Your kingdom come, your will be done, on earth as it is in heaven" (Matthew 6:10). This is a prayer for God to rule in and through our own lives, giving evidence of God our King to all those around us to the ends of the earth. Furthermore, it is a prayer for the completion of God's plan to restore all things, to bring about a perfect new heaven and new earth at the coming of the visible and eternal reign of Jesus. It is a prayer of dependence upon the plan and will of God. It is not a prayer for all our desires to be fulfilled or our dreams to come true. But instead, it is a prayer that his will be done in us, through us, and despite us. Jesus is teaching us that our prayers are to focus on God and his will.

#2. Jesus' prayer models to us that we are to bring to him our physical needs.

"Give us this day our daily bread" (Matthew 6:11). We can and must ask for our daily needs, even acknowledging that we don't always know what we most need. Sometimes we need refinement through difficulty that draws us to faith and to the Father where our needs can truly be met. So, we should pray and ask for the needs of each day. Our God cares about the individual needs of each of us! He calls us to pray and ask for provision which he wants to provide. This is a prayer of dependence resting in him and not our own strength and provision. It is a prayer for daily bread, not for provisions for the month, the year but for that day. The plan God is working out in our lives is a daily thing which takes a lifetime to be accomplished. We need to rest in the Lord for his daily provisions and trust that his daily provision is enough. It is said that a marathon is not run in miles but in steps, one step at a time. And so, we are to pray. May we live faithfully in this day, in this moment of our lives and pray, "Give us this day, our daily bread."

#3. Jesus teaches us to bring our spiritual needs to God.

"Forgive us our debts, as we also have forgiven our debtors" (Matthew 6:12a). This prayer is not for ultimate justification and righteousness (being made holy and acceptable) before God. This is not the initial prayer of repentance (turning from ourselves and sin) and faith in Jesus. Instead this is our daily prayer of repentance, seeking forgiveness and restoration in our relationship with God because of our daily sins and rebellion against his design & rule. Jesus continues, "...as we also have forgiven our debtors" (Matthew 6:12b). As a believer in Jesus who has been forgiven, we are then to forgive others. If we harbor bitterness and un-forgiveness against others, we are holding on to unconfessed sin which hinders our fellowship with God. The final spiritual need that Jesus models for us to pray for is protection from temptation and sin. This is a prayer for safety from falling into trials at the hand of Satan and this fallen world; a prayer for protection from the sin and evil that wages war against us daily. We know it, feel it and battle it so we take up the prayer of watchfulness. We acknowledge in prayer our great need of a Savior and our trust that he will provide, protect, and help even in temptation.

As we have seen, Jesus' teaching through the Lord's Prayer provides us a guide as we pray. We are to look first to God as we lift up prayers of praise for who he is and thanksgiving for all he has done and is doing. We also are to bring petitions to God for our physical and spiritual needs, and those of others. We come with humble hearts of repentance for our daily sin and dependence upon him to protect and strengthen us in coming temptation and trials. All of this we pray to our God who is our loving, holy Father in whose plan we entrust ourselves.

So pray! Pray often to the audience of our God! Pray in public and in private. Pray in silence and with a loud voice. Pray for God's glory and for your daily needs. Pray for the physical and spiritual needs of those around you. Pray and enter into a growing fellowship with your Father. Pray!

DISCUSSION QUESTIONS

1. How would you describe your prayer life?

2. What posture does God call us to take when we pray? How does this affect our prayers?

3. As we pray in all circumstances, what characteristics of God do we see?

Chapter 15

WHAT DOES IT MEAN TO BE A JOYFUL CHRISTIAN?

Mat Leonard

"Rejoice in the Lord always, I will say it again: Rejoice!"
– Philippians 4:4

Christian joy is simple. Worldly joy is complicated. Joy, if you were to google joy, the first thing that comes up is this definition: "a feeling of great pleasure and happiness."[1] This definition isn't too far from the biblical one because the biblical definition says that we find feelings of great pleasure and happiness in God through a relationship with Jesus Christ. Christian joy leaves us fulfilled and satisfied, whereas worldly joy leaves us empty, desperate, and confused. In order to understand what Christian joy is and why we are called to "Rejoice in the Lord always", we first need to understand the difference between Christian joy and worldly joy.

Worldly Joy

Imagine yourself in the workplace doing what you are passionate about. And not only are you passionate about your work, you are excelling and all the while your coworkers are praising you for how awesome you are. Your boss is also pleased and has given you a considerable raise, which is perfect timing because you have been looking at purchasing a new house right on a nearby lake with a private dock. Can you feel the joy associated with your circumstances? Do you feel great pleasure and happiness? If this joy attached to your external circumstances is what helps keep you happy, this is worldly joy.

Worldly joy is finding feelings of great pleasure and happiness solely in your external circumstances and this kind of joy is temporary. Worldly joy is temporary because our external circumstances can change from good to bad in the blink of an eye.

When we find ourselves in a bad circumstance, we often can feel frustrated, anxious, angry, and bitter, which rob us of any joy that was present. Consequently, with any negative emotions present, our tendency is to self-medicate with many different worldly pleasures or even the pursuit of what it was that was previously causing us worldly joy.

Think back to the scenario of the positive circumstances within your workplace. Now imagine that you have made some pretty significant mistakes at work and instead of being praised by your coworkers, you are being attacked. Your boss is angry and is threatening to fire you. The promotion and raise that you received has been taken away, which means you are now having to back out of the contract from buying your dream home. What are your feelings at the thought of this? What would you do if your once perfect and orderly world became completely disorienting and out of control?

If worldly joy is the only thing that you have experienced, then you will most likely put all of your effort into trying to change your external circumstances to match up with how they once were. Which means that you are going to have to try really hard to get everybody to like you again, which probably means working excessive hours to make up for the mistakes, proving to everyone how awesome you are again. This could also mean pushing back from time with friends and family, sacrificing sleep, cutting corners at work which compromises your integrity, all in the pursuit of worldly joy. When worldly joy is all you have, you will find yourself exhausted and constantly attempting to control things to keep the feelings of pleasure and happiness alive.

One of the ways we are tempted to attain worldly joy is through self-medicating with worldly activities. These self-medicating activities promise comfort and safety when really, all they do is help us escape reality and leave us empty. Plus, the more we run to these things, the more we need to run to them to help us feel joyful again. Some examples of worldly activities are: substance abuse, like alcohol or drugs; media use, such as Facebook or Netflix; or a hobby, like working out or reading books. Not all of these things in and of themselves are bad things, however, when they are used to help us try and stay joyful in life without ever looking to Jesus, we will never be fully satisfied.

Christian Joy

Christian joy, on the other hand, is qualitatively different and is not dependent on external circumstances. Christian joy has implications directly tied to the gospel, with the gospel as the foundation. This foundation of the gospel is a relationship with God through Jesus Christ and is secure and protected. Our most fundamental needs have been met through the gospel. Insecurities are replaced with confidence that is found in God's forgiveness and acceptance of us because the punishment for sin was taken care of by Jesus and his morally perfect life is credited to us as a gift! Our need for intimacy is met by being completely known by God, which allows us to be vulnerable and secure in relation with him and others around us.

Christian joy is always available to the believer no matter what the external circumstances may be because God and his truth never change and his Spirit lives within us. The gospel frees us to live lives where we can find feelings of pleasure and happiness in all seasons of life. Through the gospel we are given new eyes to see the realities of God's mercy and grace everyday. Through the gospel, we are given the Holy Spirit who resides within us as a guarantee of the inheritance we will fully receive when Jesus returns and who also transforms us to be more and more like Jesus. This is all incredible news! However, theory alone is useless unless it is put into practice. So then, what does a joyful Christian look like?

A joyful Christian is an anxiety-free Christian.

Paul writes in Philippians 4:4, "Rejoice in the Lord always. I will say it again: Rejoice!" If you are like me, I say to myself, "Really? Rejoice always? Did you really mean to write 'always'? Maybe it's just a bad translation…" However, when you look at the Greek word for "always", it actually means always. The reason this seems almost impossible is because of what you and I most likely deal with on a daily or weekly basis: An anxiety, worry ridden society that is so fast-paced and busy that being still and listening for God's voice can be difficult if we aren't constantly communing in relationship with him. Or, our lives are upside down in circumstances and we are so anxious and worried with what is going on that we run to everything else but God to medicate our feelings and emotions to feel joy.

Anxiety is a joy killer, which makes "rejoicing always" really hard to do.

So, what do we do with the exhortation to "Rejoice always"? Great question! Though it may feel like Paul raises the expectation bar really high, if we read on verse 5 shows us that we need to be gentle to all, more specifically to those who would treat you poorly. We do this because the Lord is near. So, to rejoice always means we love our enemies because our calling is to live lives that display the gospel to all even to our enemies. The gospel is found in this way of living because at one point, we were enemies, too. We were enemies to God, yet while we were still sinners he died for us (Romans 5:8).

Now you may be asking yourself, what does being gentle to all, have to do with anxiety? The Greek word for gentle is *epieikes* and "was often used of an attitude of kindness where the normal or expected response was retaliation."[2] Think about when someone wrongs you, what are the feelings that spring up? Anxiety can definitely be one of them, along with anger, worry, and betrayal, which when acted upon in retaliation helps us to medicate anxiety and takes our eyes off of Jesus, making us forget the gospel. However, when we forgive those who wrong us, as Christ Jesus forgave us (Ephesians 4:32), our anxiety decreases. In return, we then can love those who are hard to love. In this gospel response to all people, God is glorified and joy is found.

Something else that needs to be highlighted in Philippians 4 is the end of verse 5, "The Lord is near." This is an amazing truth that should give us much joy when we live with the mindset that the Lord is near! If you have placed your faith in Christ this is 100% true for you. He is so near that he is in you through the Holy Spirit. How much closer can you get? With that being true, oh what joy we can have! And not only is he in us, he promises that he will never leave us nor forsake us (Hebrews 13:5) and he is also at work within us making (Philippians 2:13) us more like Jesus. This creates an environment for great joy that can be always present. Most importantly, Christian joy can be present in the worst of times. Paul goes on to write in verse 6, "Do not be anxious about anything…"

Like Paul writes in verse 4 about rejoicing, he uses an all-encompassing word "always" when using the word "anything". He says this because he knows that anxiety kills the joy we should always have in Christ. After all, anxiety caused by adversity comes from a disbelief or distrust of God's character. It comes from thinking that we will not be taken care of in some way or another and is rooted in fear. Paul then instructs what to do when there is anxiety present with the rest of verse 6, "but in every situation, by prayer and petition, with thanksgiving, present your requests to God."

Prayer is vital to being a joyful and anxiety-free Christian. I would go so far to say that without prayer, Christian joy will not be found. Prayer keeps us in communion with God who is the source of our joy no matter what the circumstances. Just as you cannot find joy in a relationship with a friend or spouse without spending time together, the same is true with Jesus! And when anxiety presents itself, Paul instructs us to have a certain posture of prayer, one of gratitude. Think about times when you were truly grateful for something. How did you feel – happy, content, peaceful? In Christ, there are endless reasons to be grateful! I encourage you that before you start praying for God to change a situation, behold the glory of Christ by thinking about the gospel and be thankful to him for its many implications.

The battlefield of anxiety is in our minds. Anxiety will put blinders up and will try to keep you from seeing the glorious reality of the gospel by making you focus on whatever is making you anxious. However, when we take those thoughts captive and subject them to Christ (2 Corinthians 10:5), it will clear our mind to see what is really true in our lives when it comes to gospel implications and how awesome Jesus really is. Paul gives us a way to do this in his final exhortation in Philippians 4:8, "...whatever is true, whatever is noble, whatever is right, whatever is pure, whatever is lovely, whatever is admirable—if anything is excellent or praiseworthy—think about such things." Christian, Jesus meets all of these qualifiers in our thought life! So, if you are having anxiety and are having a hard time being grateful in your prayers to God, think about Jesus! Thank Jesus, pray to Jesus, praise Jesus for what he has done for you and what he is doing in you! Think about Jesus! Do it! Do it now, and joy will surely come for to be a joyful Christian is to be an anxiety-free Christian.

A joyful Christian is an obedient Christian.

In order to understand that to be a joyful Christian is to be an obedient Christian, we must look at the perfect example in Christ's obedience to the Father as he was led to the cross. This will show us that even when obedience leads to suffering, joy is still found in obeying God because we are in relationship with him and he delights in our obedience. In Matthew 26:36-46 we find Jesus overwhelmed with sorrow, to the point of death, praying and asking the Father to "let this cup pass from" him. What he was speaking of was the cross where he would take on the wrath of God for the sins of humanity. Three times he pleads for the cup to pass yet he prays "not my will but yours be done." How can Jesus be content with the Father's will to drink the cup of wrath? Jesus could do this because he understood that great joy is found in doing the Father's will and when we are pursuing God's will, we can be assured that this pleases him. Pleasing God provides us with so much joy, for creation longs to be delighted in by its Creator.

Hebrews 12:2 further paints the picture of the joy Jesus found in the midst of extreme suffering caused by obedience by saying, "for the joy that was set before him he endured the cross." This shows us that joy is not only found in obedience, but joy is the motivator for obedience. John Piper writes in his book *Desiring God*,

> I think there was joy in Gethsemane as Jesus was led away—not fun, not sensual pleasure, not laughter, in fact not anything that this world can offer. But there was a good feeling deep in Jesus' heart that his action was pleasing to his Father, and that the reward to come would outweigh all the pain. This profoundly good feeling is the joy that enabled Jesus to do for us what he did.[3]

Joy is what fuels our obedience and joy is what is found in obedience. Think of it this way – to obey God is to love him (1 John 5:3), and we love him because he first loved us (1 John 4:19). Because God first loved us, we can see how good he is by looking at Jesus! Therefore, in his perfect goodness, we can trust that when he asks us to do something, it is for his glory and for our good.

For example, God commands us to obey him by being sexually pure. As a Christian, we understand that this command can be extremely difficult, especially in a season of dating, engagement, or courtship because passions run high and the desire to express this passion sexually can be tempting and painful, right? Not only are we tempted to express the passion, but we are tempted to think about it. So, to obey God in his command to be sexually pure is to take him at his Word that he knows what is best for us. And if we are blessed with a covenant marriage, we are still commanded to have sexual purity within marriage by honoring the marriage bed and remaining faithful to that person as long as you both live, which gives us great joy and honors God. And whether we are blessed with a marriage covenant or we are blessed to be single, the ultimate joy is found when we trust that God is better than sex will ever be and a relationship with him is better than any we have here on this earth.

Disobeying God and his Word hinders our relationship with him. When we disobey God, shame follows and robs us of joy, causing us to run and hide from the source of joy just as Adam and

Eve hid from God in the garden. Through Jesus and the gospel, this shame doesn't have to keep us away from him. Because of Jesus, he reminds us daily that we can flee from sin and walk in obedience again where joy is found. To be a joyful Christian is to be an obedient Christian because an obedient Christian is a Christian who loves God and trusts his ways are always good. Did you hear that? God and his ways are always good so, lovingly obey him!

Conclusion

There is much more to be said about what it means to be a joyful Christian but at the root of Christian joy is the enjoyment of a life saved by Jesus. From this, we experience him in prayer, through the Bible, and in Christian community. Would we all as Christians pursue joy in Jesus because we are all ultimately longing for his fulfillment. John Piper says it best:

> Christian Hedonism is the conviction that God's ultimate goal in the world (his glory) and our deepest desire (to be happy) are one and the same, because *God is most glorified in us when we are most satisfied in him*. Not only is God the supreme source of satisfaction for the human soul, but God himself is glorified by our being satisfied in him. Therefore, our pursuit of joy in him is essential.[4]

DISCUSSION QUESTIONS

1. What are the main differences between worldly joy & Christian joy?

2. In what worldly ways are you tempted to satisfy your longing for joy?

3. What can you do to increase your joy & delight & satisfaction in Christ?

Chapter 16

IF I AM SAVED BY GRACE, WHY DOES IT MATTER HOW I LIVE?

Gabe Reed

> The chief end of man is to glorify God and enjoy him forever.
> *– The Westminster Confession of Faith*

Christians need to answer the "why questions." Our joy and passion to follow Jesus wanes the longer we put off answering the question: "Why does it matter how I live?" Let's assume that we're answering it from a Christian perspective, rooted in grace. My salvation depends on grace (Ephesians 2:8-10), there is nothing that I can do to gain God's love. His love is a *gift*. Would you ever try to pay for a gift someone gives you? There was nothing and is nothing I do to *pay* for God's gift.

If nothing I did brought me into God's love, then, now in God's love, there must be nothing for me to do. It does not matter how I live as a Christian. Stop the presses! Take a coffee break. This question needs highly caffeinated thinking, truth from the Bible and the Holy Spirit in you. When the Spirit of God convinces you from the Bible why it matters how you live out grace, you have fuel for life as a disciple of Jesus.

Jesus teaching about God's unmerited favor had the Pharisees on full alert. They knew Jesus' grace wouldn't motivate people to follow God. Jesus missed the ball because his grace didn't have the teeth to motivate his disciples for living a godly life. The religious leaders in Jesus' day knew how to make people dance to their tune, lay on as much guilt, point to your own self-pride and tell them to get to work. After all, grace is a permission slip to have a field day of sinful pleasure. The Pharisee in each of us might be tempted to leave grace, but there is a far more satisfying answer: Jesus spurs us on in a life of receiving grace and living by faith.

Grace and God's glory change our motivation for living. God's grace changes us in a way that restores us to our purpose, glorifying God. God's honorable reputation then becomes the answers our big life question: "Why am I alive today? What's my purpose?" If you are rescued by Jesus, it was for this primary purpose, to show forth the bright and glorious identity of God. God ties your life to his own reputation and honor when he calls you to faith in Jesus and gives you every gift of heaven in his Son.

The Glory of Jesus

In 2 Thessalonians 2:13, Paul says,

> But we ought to always give thanks to God for you, brothers beloved by the Lord, because God chose you as the first-fruits to be saved, through sanctification by the Spirit and belief in the truth. To this he called you through our gospel, so that you may obtain the glory of our Lord Jesus Christ.

First, in Christ, you are headed to Jesus' glory, you are called by God. Where Jesus is, close to his Father, you will be also. Christian, the Bible declares this is your destiny: sharing in Jesus' glory. The

Father saw fit to wrap you into the plan of making his Son known to everyone. As his redeemed, you reflect God in a special way. As a recipient of God's gracious gift you reveal him by your very own life. The world around you sees the grace of God through your life. So then, it matters how we reflect and reveal God's grace.

The New City Catechism asks this question:

Question: How can we glorify God?
Answer: We glorify God by enjoying him, loving him, trusting him, and obeying his will, commands and law.[1]

When you respond in joyful obedience the Lord out of his grace toward you, God is glorified. The best witness of God's good news is a person responding to God's grace in this way. The world should and will know this glory. Consider your life, how does God's grace in your life point others to God? If you were the only Christian that your friends, family and co-workers would see, what would your life tell them about your God? How could your life speak clearer about God's gracious love for you?

Jesus, Joy and Moses

For the sake of your own joy in God, your life choices matter. No one says, "I want a little less joy in my life. I think I might be too happy." Everyone is looking for joy and satisfaction, but not everyone is living that life to the fullest. Most people point to the crummy circumstances of their life. Not Moses, Moses' life circumstances were perfect. Yet he gave up his wealth for a joy that included all kinds of suffering, setting out on a long and arduous journey, never again having a home and surrounded continually with negative people. And if he were, he would say it was worth it! Because he suffered all those things in pursuit of his joy in Jesus.

Hebrews 11:24-26 tells us that

> by faith Moses, when he was grown up, refused to be called the son of Pharaoh's daughter, choosing rather to be mistreated with the people of God than to enjoy the fleeting pleasures of sin. He considered the reproach of Christ greater wealth than the treasures of Egypt, for he was looking to the reward.

Moses had the greatest joys the world could offer in Egypt. Being in the house of Pharaoh, he missed out on nothing. It was all there, the buffet with no dessert missing. And Moses walked away. Hebrews adds the commentary on his unique choice, that being the son of Pharaoh's daughter offered empty, short-term thrills that never truly satisfied. Instead, like Jesus, he endured being verbally abused because he was motivated by lasting joy.

John Macarthur says about Moses,

> For forty years he enjoyed the riches of Egypt. For the rest of his life, he forsook them, because they interfered with this obedience to God, and would have prevented his receiving immeasurable greater riches when it came time for eternal rewards.[2]

In the Christian's pursuit of Jesus, they say no to all kinds of lifestyle choices, opportunities to have pleasure for a moment in order to enjoy God fully and for all eternity. Life choices matter for greater, lasting joy in Jesus. The problem with people today is that they do not invest enough in joy, we are sold too easily on cheap, short pleasures, when eternal joy with God is offered before us.

I never go with my wife to buy a phone or laptop. She is a lifetime member of the Apple occult, I mean culture. Okay, not quite a full member. When I bought her an Apple watch for her birthday, she returned it. Evidently that is the marker you're not sold out completely. But she reminds when I need a computer or phone, "Don't buy cheap, buy quality, buy something like Apple." I always buy cheap and I always regret it. Even while I wrote this chapter on my "low-end limp-along laptop", it crashed. Sin offers us a deceptively short and never truly satisfying joy. It crashes as well.

Sin offers us a bargain that is always too good to be true. It brings regret after the moment. For the sake of your own satisfaction in Jesus, you make important decisions every moment with your head, heart, body and relationships. Consider the Christian guy who dates a young woman that makes him feel so good. But she does not love Jesus, not like this guy, not at all. In the moment, the decision to take the plunge into romantic entanglement seems like the greatest high in the world! Yet it plunges into the deepest lows. Yet the most insane part of sin's ordeal is still to come. In our tears we look back at Jesus and blame him for our grief. As if our choosing to not trust Jesus's clear, spelled-out-in-the-Bible direction was Jesus' fault.

The truth is, the way you live your life matters, for your joy in Jesus. All the choices in life have consequences. Moses taught us that we must give up the short-lived joys of sin in order to enjoy fellowship with Jesus. And nothing, not even pain and suffering, can steal the long-lasting joy we gain in choosing Jesus over sin.

DISCUSSION QUESTIONS

1. Who are the non-believers around you that are watching how you live?

2. How are the riches of this world interfering with your eternal rewards that are promised from God?

3. What short-lived joys is God calling you to give up? How will that increase your joy in Jesus?

CONTRIBUTORS

Jordan Branch and his wonderful wife, Jessica, have three kids: Nathan, Lillian, and Bryce. He serves as a pastor/elder at Calvary Church – Lakewood in Lakewood, CO. He enjoys time with his kids, camping, reading, sports, and playing music.

Franck Corbiere currently serves as a pastor-elder at Calvary Church - Englewood in Englewood, CO, and he has served as a missionary in Russia and France as well as Church Planter/Lead Pastor of Greater Grace Evangelical Church in Norwood, Massachusetts. Franck is married to Kathy, and their family includes, Noelle, their daughter, along with 3 foster children.

Adam Embry is one of the pastors at Calvary Church – Summitview in Centennial, CO, and he has published books in historical theology and counseling. Adam also serves as a military chaplain in the United States Air Force Reserves. He is married to Charlotte and has six children.

Dan Freng serves as Lead Pastor-Elder at Calvary Church – Littleton, in Littleton, CO. He is married to Kelly and has five kids: Noah, Jasmine, Brian, Isaac, and Shamie. Dan and his family love to travel and play sports together.

Mark Hallock serves as the Lead Pastor of Calvary Church – Englewood in Englewood, CO, and as President of the Calvary Family of Churches. Mark is a big fan of tennis, pop punk music, and good Mexican food. His favorite hobby is hanging out with his wife, Jenna, and their two kids, Zoe and Eli.

Kevin Hasenack serves as Pastor of Calvary Church - Wellspring in Aurora, CO. Kevin loves his wife of 14 years, Jenn, and their sweet daughter Charlie. He loves doing intercultural ministry and church planting, and he wants to see Jesus become a non-ignorable part of the culture in Colorado.

Dave Herre is serves as the lead replanting Pastor-Elder for Calvary Church - Derby Hill in Loveland, CO. Previously, his family spent 8 years serving in East Asia ministering in a city where less than 1% know Jesus. Dave is married to Kelly, and they have 3 wonderful children: Antheney, Caleb, & Rachel.

Mathew Leonard serves as the Lead Pastor of Calvary Church - Blanca in Blanca, CO. He is grateful for his wife, Toni, and is a father to his son, Nathaniel. He loves reading, spending time outdoors, hunting, and hiking.

Michael Morgan serves as a pastor-elder of Calvary Church - Wellspring in Aurora, CO, and as Academic Dean of William Tennent School of Theology, and he has worked in inner-city, prison, and urban church-planting ministries for the past 20 years. Whenever he gets the chance, Michael enjoys hiking in the mountains with his wife, Kate, and three amazing kids, Joshua, Abigail, and Patrick.

Gabe Reed is the Lead Pastor-Elder of Calvary Church – Summitview in Centennial, CO, and is married to Heather. Together, they have a son and daughter, Tytus and Joelle. As a family, they love Jesus and several wonders of his creation, namely mountains and zoos.

Spencer Parish serves as the planting Pastor-Elder at Calvary Church – Kearney in Kearney, NE. He loves Jesus, his gracious wife Lauren, daughter Juliet (the cutest kid in the world), and America's pastime (baseball).

Nathan Piotrowski serves as the Lead Pastor of Calvary Church - Monument in Monument, CO as well as an 8th grade English teacher at a local public school. He married to his beautiful bride, Ruth, and has three children, Lydia, Mayah, and Joel.

Evan Skelton serves as Lead Pastor of Bayless Baptist Church, a church replant in St. Louis, MO, after serving as a church planter and replanting resident with the Calvary Family of Churches. He and his wife, Grace, are loving the adventure of raising their four kids–Clara, Oliver, Arlo, and baby (coming May 2020)–while Evan finds much joy in great cups of coffee, nerdy board games, and Chipotle.

Seth Van Essen has served as a pastor-elder at Calvary Church – Englewood, in Englewood, CO. He is married to his best friend, Keely, and they are enjoying adventures with their twins–Daylin and Kellan. He fills his time with work in the business world, pastoring, family life, outdoor adventures, traveling, and finding joy in the simple things of life.

Matt Whitacre has served a pastor-elder at Calvary Church - Restoration in Aurora, CO. He is married to Leann and they have four kids: Hannah, Adelyn, Brielle and Josiah. As a family, they love to learn about other cultures and try different ethnic cuisines.

Garrett Wishall is the Associate Pastor at Calvary Church – Littleton in Littleton, CO. He is the husband of Laura and they are blessed with four children: Timothy, Alex, Luke and Hallie.

NOTES

Chapter 1. Can I really trust the Bible?

[1] Craig Blomberg, Can We Still Believe the Bible? An Evangelical Engagement with Contemporary Questions (Grand Rapids: Brazos Press, 2014), 5.

[2] Lee Strobel, The Case for Christ: A Journalist's Personal Investigation of the Evidence for Jesus (Grand Rapids: Zondervan, 1998), Kindle Edition, 58-63.

[3] Blomberg, Can We Still Believe the Bible?, 27.

[4] Paul Enns, The Moody Handbook of Theology (Chicago: Moody Bible Institute, 1989), 155.

[5] Christopher Wright, The Mission of God: Unlocking the Bible's Grand Narrative (Downers Grove: InterVarsity Press, 2006), 48. "Canon" refers to the 66 books of the Bible.

[6] "Scripture Access Statistics," Wycliffe Global Alliance, accessed July 28, 2018, http://www.wycliffe.net/statistics.

[7] For a longer discussion on the truthfulness of Scripture, see the International Council on Biblical Inerrancy, "The Chicago Statement on Biblical Inerrancy," accessed July 20, 2018, http://library.dts.edu/Pages/TL/Special/ICBI_1.pdf.

[8] See John 3:16-17, 14:25-26; Romans 6:3-11; Hebrews 10:10-14

[9] Sally Lloyd-Jones, The Jesus Storybook Bible (Grand Rapids: Zonderkidz, 2007), 14.

Chapter 2. Why is the Bible so violent but Jesus is so loving?

[1] Richard Dawkins, *The God Delusion* (New York: Houghton Mifflin Company, 2006), 31.

[2] "Stories of Violence," in *Dictionary of Biblical Imagery*, eds. Leland Ryken, James C. Wilhoit, Tremper Longman III (Downers Grove, IL: InterVarsity Press, 1998), 917.

[3] Christopher Hitchens, *God is not Great* (Hatchette Book Group: New York, 2007), 100.

[4] Sometimes the issue of multiple wives comes up when discussing biblical sexual ethics. Were Israel's patriarchs and kings allowed to have multiple wives? Certainly not. Genesis 2:24 also forms the sexual standard for Israel's kings in Deut 17:17. Nothing good for the family ever comes from having multiple wives.

[5] Just food for thought, but given sexual immortality and sexual violence, it's of no insignificance that the Messiah is born to a virgin.

[6] John Wolffe, *The Expansion of Evangelicalism: The Age of Wilberforce, More, Chalmers and Finney* (Downers Grove, IL: Intervarsity Press, 2007), 197-98.

[7] Sean McDowell and Jonathan Morrow, eds., *Is God Just a Human Invention? And Seventeen Other Questions Raised by the New Atheists* (Grand Rapids: Kregel Publications, 2010), 177.

[8] James M. Hamilton, Jr., *God's Glory in Salvation Through Judgment: A Biblical Theology* (Wheaton, IL: Crossway, 2010), 57.

[9] Hamilton, 59.

[10] Kevin J. Vanhoozer, "The Atonement in Postmodernity: Guild, Goats, and Gifts," *The Glory of the Atonement*, ed. Charles E. Hill and Frank A. James III (Downers Grove, IL: Intervarsity Press, 2004), 398-401.

[11] John Webster, *Confronted by Grace: Meditations of a Theologian* (Bellingham, WA: Lexham Press, 2015), 85-86.

Chapter 3. Is Jesus really the only way to be saved?

[1] Frank Newport, "Mississippi Most Religious State, Vermont Least Religious," *Gallup*, accessed April 14, 2020, https://news.gallup.com/poll/167267/mississippi-religious-vermont-least-religious-state.aspx?utm_source=alert&utm_medium=email&utm_campaign=syndication&utm_content=morelink&utm_term=All%20Gallup%20Headlines%20-%20Religion#1. Colorado was 38th in a poll of most religious states in America. Religious News Service, "Poll: Colorado ranks low in weekly church attendance," *The Gazette*, accessed April 14, 2020, https://gazette.com/life/poll-colorado-ranks-low-in-weekly-church-attendance/article_6c9b2f8e-cd83-52c2-9fcc-1d38f237631c.html. 25% of Colorado residents attend religious services on a weekly basis, in the bottom 10 in America.

[2] International Council on Biblical Inerrancy, "The Chicago Statement on Biblical Inerrancy," accessed July 20, 2018, http://www.bible-researcher.com/chicago1.html.

³ John MacArthur *Why One Way? Defending an Exclusive Claim in an Inclusive World* (Nashville: W Publishing Group, 2002). MacArthur's book was helpful as a resource on the matter of biblical authority as it relates to why Jesus is the only way to God.

⁴ "The Baptist Faith and Message 2000," *Southern Baptist Convention*, accessed April 14, 202, http://www.sbc.net/bfm2000/bfm2000.asp.

Chapter 4. How can I comprehend that God is three-in-one?

¹ "A Prayer to the Triune God," *Valley of Vision*, Ed. by Arthur Bennett (Edinburgh, Scotland: The Banner of Truth Trust, 1975).

² Deut. 6:4, compared to 4:35, 39; 1 Kings 8:60; Isa. 45:5f.

³ Henry C. Thiessen, *Lectures in Systematic Theology* (Grand Rapids, MI: Eerdmans Publishing Company, 1986), 89.

⁴ Ibid, 90

⁵ John M. Frame, *Systematic Theology: An Introduction to Christian Belief* (Philipsburg, PA.: P&R Publishing, 2013), 483.

⁶ Ibid, 484.

⁷ Needs citation

⁸ John M. Frame, *Salvation Belongs to the Lord, An Introduction to Systematic Theology* (Philipsburg, PA.: P&R Publishing, 2006), p. 36.

⁹ *The New Catechism Devotional* (Wheaton, IL: Crossway, 2017), 25.

¹⁰ Ibid., 36

¹¹ Eric Mascall, quoted in Peter Toon, *Yesterday, Today and Forever* (Swedesboro, NJ: Preservation, 1996), 210.

Chapter 5. Can I love Jesus but not the church?

¹ "According to aggregate Barna tracking data, this group makes up one-tenth of the population, and it's growing (up from 7% in 2004)." "Meet Those Who 'Love Jesus but Not the Church,'" *Barna Group* (March 30, 2017), accessed August 8, 2018, https://www.barna.com/research/meet-love-jesus-not-church/.

² Catherine L. Morgan, *Thirty Thousand Days: The Journey Home to God* (Fearn, Ross-shire: Christian Focus, 2016), 111-112.

[3] Rick Warren, "Living the Purpose Driven Life" (message presented at Campus Crusade for Christ Summer Staff Training Conference, July 2003).

[4] Michael Reeves, *Delighting in the Trinity: An Introduction to the Christian Faith* (Downers Grove, IL: IVP Academic, 2012), 28.

[5] John Newton, *The Works of John Newton*, ed. Richard Cecil (Edinburgh: Banner of Truth Trust, 1988), 1:269.

Chapter 6. *How do I find the right church?*

[1] Primary doctrines are those that are essential to historic, orthodox Christianity. Moving away from these core truths means moving away from biblical Christianity. Secondary doctrines are those that, while important, are not essential for matters pertaining to salvation and/or orthodoxy.

Chapter 7. Why do we celebrate the Lord's Supper every week?

[1] Thomas Watson, "The Holy Eucharist; or the Mystery of the Lord's Supper Briefly Explained," *The Writings of the Doctrinal Puritans and Divines of the Seventeenth Century* (Religious Tract Society, 1848), 6.

[2] Eckhard J. Schnabel, *Exegetical Commentary on the New Testament: Volume 5, Acts* (Grand Rapids, MI: Zondervan, 2012), 179.

Chapter 8. How do I engage practically in the mission of God?

[1] Michelle Warren, *The Power of Proximity* (Downers Grove, IL: InterVarsity Press, 2017), 25.

[2] Carl Mederias, *42 Seconds* (Carol Stream, IL: Tyndale House Publishers, 2018), 2.

[3] Jay Pathak and David Runyon, *The Art of Neighboring* (Grand Rapids, MI: Baker Books, 2012).

Chapter 9. What is my role in global missions?

[1] Stephen McCaskell, *Through the Eyes of C.H. Spurgeon* (Brenham, TX: Lucid Books, 2012), 124.

[2] Andy Johnson, *Missions: How the Local Church Goes Global* (Wheaton: Crossway, 2017), 14.

[3] John Piper, *Let the Nations Be Glad!: The Supremacy of God in Missions* (Nottingham, England: Inter-Varsity Press, 2010), 17.

[4] Jason Mandryk and Patrick J. St. G. Johnstone, *Operation World* (Colorado Springs, CO: Biblica Publishing, 2010), 21.

[5] J. Mack. Stiles, *Evangelism: How the Whole Church Speaks of Jesus* (Wheaton, IL: Crossway, 2014), 81.

[6] Jeff Lewis, *Gods Heart for the Nations* (Littleton, CO: Caleb Project, 2002), 6.

[7] Stephen McCaskell, *Through the Eyes of C.H. Spurgeon*, 122.

Chapter 10. What does the Bible have to say about social justice?

[1] Timothy Keller, *Generous Justice: How God's Grace Makes Us Just* (New York: Riverhead Books, 2012), 5.

[2] Rodney Stark, *The Rise of Christianity: How the Obscure, Marginal Jesus Movement Became the Dominant Religious Force in the Western World in a Few Centuries* (San Francisco, CA: HarperSanFrancisco, 1997), 83-88.

[3] John Piper, *The Swans Are Not Silent, vol. 3, The Roots of Endurance: Invincible Perseverance in the Lives of John Newton, Charles Simeon, and William Wilberforce* (Wheaton, Ill.: Crossway Books, 2002), 17.

[4] Kevin DeYoung and Greg Gilbert, *What Is the Mission of the Church? Making Sense of Social Justice, Shalom, and the Great Commission* (Wheaton, Ill.: Crossway, 2011), 177.

[5] Timothy Keller, *Generous Justice: How God's Grace Makes Us Just* (New York: Riverhead Books, 2012), 82.

Chapter 11. If I gave my life to Jesus, why is my life so hard?

[1] Mez McConnell, "Why Is the Christian Life So Hard?" *20 Schemes Blog*, accessed August 15, 2018, https://20schemes.com/us/2017/05/why-is-the-christian-life-so-hard-an-excerpt-from-war-why-did-life-just-get-harder/.

Chapter 12. Why does God care about my sex life?

[1] The consistent testimony of the Bible, it turns out, is that marriage was made to picture this fundamental love relationship, particularly in sex. In sex in this context, two people, a man and a wife, disclose and commit themselves to the other, binding them together in much more than a physical sense. They are bound together so intimately that this couple can be spoken of not as two but as "one flesh" (Genesis 2:24).

[2] This phrase is used often by Timothy Keller in summarizing the gospel.

[3] Jackie Hill Perry, *Gay Girl, Good God*, Kindle Edition (Nashville: B&H Publishing Group).

Chapter 13. How can I be more Christ-like in my communication?

[1] Robert D. Jones, *Uprooting Anger: Biblical Help for A Common Problem* (Phillipsburg, NJ: P & R, 2005), 12.

[2] C. S. Lewis, *Mere Christianity* (London: Harper Collins, 1977), 101.

[3] Charles Wesley, "And Can It Be" (No. 147) in The Baptist Hymnal (Nashville: Convention Press, 1991).

Chapter 14. How can I improve my prayer life?

[1] RC Sproul, *Essential Truths of The Christian Faith* (Wheaton: Tyndale House Publishers, Inc., 1992), 251.

[2] N.T. Wright, "The Lord's Prayer as a Paradigm of Christian Prayer," *NTWrightPage*, accessed July 25, 2018, http://ntwrightpage.com/2016/07/12/the-lords-prayer-as-a-paradigm-of-christian-prayer/.

[3] Wayne Grudem, *Systematic Theology: An Introduction to Biblical Doctrine* (Grand Rapids: Zondervan Publishing House, 1994), 376.

[4] R.A. Torrey, *The Power of Prayer and the Prayer of Power* (1924; repr., New York: Cosmo Classics, 2009), 61.

Chapter 15. What does it mean to be a joyful Christian?

[1] *Lexico*, s.v. "joy," accessed April 17, 2020, https://www.lexico.com/en/definition/joy.

[2] Frank Thielman, *Philippians: from Biblical Text-- to Contemporary Life*, The NIV Application Commentary Series (Grand Rapids, Mich.: Zondervan Pub. House, 1995), 218.

[3] John Piper, *Desiring God: Meditations of a Christian Hedonist*, 25th ed. (Colorado Springs, Colo.: Multnomah, 2011), 135.

[4] John Piper, "Joy is not optional. It's essential," *Desiring God*, assessed August 15, 2018 https://www.desiringgod.org/topics/christian-hedonism

Chapter 16. If I am saved by grace, why does it matter how I live?

[1] *The New City Catechism* (Wheaton: Crossway, 2017), 26-27.

[2] John MacArthur, *Hebrews*, The MacArthur New Testament Commentary Series (Chicago: Moody Press, 1983), 355.

SOLA

five 16th-century truths that recaptured the heart of the gospel and why they matter today

Mark Hallock & Ben Haley

Welcome to the Family is an insider's look into the Calvary Family of Churches (CFC)—its core values and doctrines are on full display as multiple authors ranging from church pastors and members to planters and replanters come together to form a united vision for the church. Readers will find the contents to be thought-provoking and informative, helping those curious about the CFC to understand ***(and perhaps join)*** the vision and hope of the movement.

EDITED BY
MARK HALLOCK

acomapress.org

ACOMA PRESS

Acoma Press exists to make Jesus non-ignorable by equipping and encouraging churches through gospel-centered resources.

Toward this end, each purchase of an Acoma Press resource serves to catalyze disciple-making and to equip leaders in God's Church. In fact, a portion of your purchase goes directly to funding planting and replanting efforts in North America and beyond. To see more of our current resources, visit us at *acomapress.org*.

Thank you.

www.ingramcontent.com/pod-product-compliance
Lightning Source LLC
Chambersburg PA
CBHW060155050426
42446CB00013B/2836